A Latin Grammar

A Latin Grammar

James Morwood

OXFORD
UNIVERSITY PRESS

Great Clarendon Street, Oxford OX2 6DP

Oxford University Press is a department of the University of Oxford.
It furthers the University's objective of excellence in research, scholarship,
and education by publishing worldwide in

Oxford New York

Athens Auckland Bangkok Bogotá Buenos Aires Calcutta
Cape Town Chennai Dar es Salaam Delhi Florence Hong Kong Istanbul
Karachi Kuala Lumpur Madrid Melbourne Mexico City Mumbai
Nairobi Paris São Paulo Singapore Taipei Tokyo Toronto Warsaw

with associated companies in Berlin Ibadan

Published in the United States
by Oxford University Press Inc., New York

First published 1999

Benjamin Hall Kennedy's Memory Rhymes reprinted by permission of
Pearson Education Limited.

British Library Cataloguing in Publication Data

Data available

Library of Congress Cataloging in Publication Data

Data available

ISBN 0-19-860277-4

10 9 8 7 6 5 4 3 2 1

Typeset in Slimbach, Meta and Trade Gothic
by Alliance Phototypesetters, India
Printed in the United States of America
on acid-free paper

Contents

Introduction

This grammar is intended for everyone with an interest in Latin. While most of it should be accessible to near-beginners, it is hoped that those in their later years at school, as well as undergraduates and mature adults, will find it a good guide. It aims to be a 'primer' (a first book) and at the same time something more than that. It aspires in fact, however inadequately, to be a new Kennedy (*The Revised Latin Primer* by Benjamin Hall Kennedy) for the new millennium. It may smack of *hubris* to lay claim to the tradition established by the author of so trusty a book which has served so many generations so very well, especially in the impeccable revision of Sir James Mountford (1930). Yet, magnificently comprehensive though the revised Kennedy was, there are simply too many charts and too many exceptions for today's Latinist, who is unlikely to have the time to learn that the accusative and ablative endings of *sēmentis* (sowing) are different from those of *cīuis* (citizen), and may feel that there are more important principal parts to be mastered than those of *sarciō* (I patch).

A further point is that Kennedy would never have claimed that he offered more than a skeletal account of the many Latin constructions. I have attempted to lay out a fairly full and, as I hope, user-friendly analysis of them. To these analyses I have added sentences from both Latin into English and English into Latin through which users of this grammar can practise what they are learning, and I have included vocabularies which will not only make these exercises easier but will also make possible a detailed examination of the Latin sentences given as examples in the explanatory parts of the book.

I am delighted to have compiled the first Latin grammar in English to have banished the letter 'v' from the Latin alphabet. It was never there.

Acknowledgements

It is a pleasure to acknowledge the generous help I have received from many quarters. Sidney Allen, Denis Feeney, Gregory Hutchinson, Peter Pormann and Kim Richardson have made valuable contributions. John Penney gave magisterial guidance in a particularly tricky section.

Five individuals call for particular gratitude. Rachel Chapman saw to the production of the manuscript of the bulk of this book, her considerable skills proving more than equal to the scrawls with which I defaced the recurrent revisions. Maurice Balme is responsible for the basic lay-out of the grammar tables, which derive from those in our Oxford Latin Course. David Langslow, Ted Kenney and Ian McAuslan have been lavish of their seemingly limitless expertise in their detailed critiques of the entire manuscript. I have benefited more than I can say from their guidance. I hope that they will forgive me for the passages that remain where the demands of clarity have led me to be economical with the truth, and those in which misunderstanding or simple carelessness has caused me to remain mired in error. For these I take full responsibility.

James Morwood
Wadham College, Oxford

Glossary of grammatical terms

ablative   a case with the basic meanings of 'by', 'with', 'from', 'at', 'in' or 'on'; some prepositions take the ablative.

accusative   the usual case of a direct object; many prepositions take the accusative.

active   the form of a verb used when the subject of the sentence is the doer of the action: we saw = uīdimus.

adjective   a word describing a noun, with which it agrees in gender and number: a *happy* girl = puella *laeta*.

adverb   a word that describes or changes the meaning of a verb, an adjective or another adverb: he walks *slowly* = *lentē* ambulat.

agree   are in the same case and number as

antecedent   is the noun or pronoun to which a relative pronoun refers back.

aorist tense the tense of a verb that refers to something that happened in the past: I *did* this = hoc *fēcī*. (Compare the perfect tense, in which the word 'have' or 'has' is used in English.)

cardinals   see numerals.

case   the form of a noun, pronoun, adjective or article that shows the part it plays in a sentence; there are six cases: nominative, vocative, accusative, genitive, dative and ablative.

clause   a self-contained section of a sentence in which there are at least a subject and a verb.

common   either masculine or feminine according to meaning.

comparative   the form of an adjective or adverb that makes it mean *more*, *rather* or *too*: more old (older), rather old, too old = *senior*.

complement   a word of phrase which describes the subject of the verb; it is used with verbs such as 'I am' and 'I become' which cannot take an object: my sister is *intelligent* = soror mea *sapiēns* est.

compound verb a verb formed by adding a prefix to a simple verb: I *pro*pose = *prō*pōnō.

concessive clause a clause usually beginning with the word 'although' or 'though'.

conditional clause a clause usually beginning with the words 'if', 'if not' or 'unless'.

conjugate give the different forms of the verb: e.g. am*ā*s = *you* love; ām*ā*u*ē*runt = *they* lov*ed*.

conjugation there are four main patterns according to which most Latin verbs change their endings; we call these 'conjugations'.

conjunction a word used to join clauses, phrases or words together: pāx *et* imperium = peace *and* empire.

consonant a letter representing a sound that can only be used together with a vowel such as b, c, d: see vowel.

dative the case of an indirect object; among its many meanings are 'to' and 'for'.

declension there are five main patterns according to which most Latin nouns change their endings; we call these 'declensions'.

decline go through the different cases of a noun, adjective or pronoun, in order.

definite article in English, 'the'. There is no definite article in Latin.

deliberative showing that a thought process is going on: What am I to do?

deponent verb a verb which is passive in form but active in meaning

direct object the noun or pronoun directly affected by the verb: he killed *the king* = r*ē*gem interf*ē*cit.

direct speech the words actually used by a speaker.

distributives see numerals.

ending letters added to the the stem of verbs, nouns and adjectives, according to tense, case, etc.

feminine one of the three genders: f*ē*mina = a woman.

finite verb a verb in a tense, as opposed to infinitives and participles.

future perfect tense the tense of a verb that refers to something in the future at a stage after it has happened: I *shall have* done this: hoc *fēcerō*.

future tense the tense of a verb that refers to something that will happen in the future.

gender the class in which a noun or pronoun is placed in a grammatical grouping; in both English and Latin, these classes are masculine, feminine, neuter, and common (i.e. either masculine or feminine according to meaning).

genitive the case that shows possession; among its many meanings the dominant one is 'of'.

gerund a verbal noun: the art *of* ruling = ars *regendī*.

gerundive a verbal adjective, frequently expressing the idea of obligation: this *must-be-done* = hoc *faciendum* est.

imperative the parts of the verb that express a command: hurry up! = festīnā!

imperfect tense the tense which expresses continuous or repeated or incomplete action in the past: I *was* walk*ing* = ambulā*bam*.

impersonal verb a verb introduced in English by the word 'it', and in Latin found only in the 3rd person singular: it rains = pluit.

indeclinable refers to a noun or adjective which never varies.

indefinite article in English, 'a' or 'an'. There is no indefinite article in Latin.

indicative refers to a verb when it makes a statement or asks a question: he said this = hoc dīxit. In a Latin grammar, the main use of this word is to indicate that the verb is not in the subjunctive.

indirect command the reporting of an actual command: e.g. 'Do this' (direct speech, direct command), She instructed him *to do this* (indirect command).

indirect object   the noun or pronoun indirectly affected by the verb, at which the direct object is aimed: I gave *him* the book = librum *eī* dedī.

indirect question   the reporting of an actual question: e.g. 'What are you doing?' (direct speech, direct question), I asked her *what she was doing* (indirect question).

indirect statement   the reporting of someone's actual words: e.g. 'I have done this' (direct speech), He said *that he had done this* (indirect speech).

infinitive   a verbal noun, the basic part of a verb: to love = amāre.

inflection   see ending.

interjection   a sound, word or phrase standing outside the grammatical structure of the sentence and expressing an emotion such as anger, fear, distress or joy: alas! = ēheu!

intransitive verb   a verb which does not take a direct object: e.g. 'go', 'come'.

irregular verb   a verb that does not follow one of the set patterns (i.e. is not in one of the four conjugations) and has its own individual forms.

jussive   giving an order.

locative   the case which tells us where something is happening, e.g. domī = at home

main clause   the clause which is the basic grammatical unit of a sentence. 'Although I hate him, he still chases me.' 'He still chases me' makes sense on its own, while 'although I hate him' does not. Thus 'He still chases me' is the main clause, and 'athough I hate him' is a subordinate clause.

masculine   one of the three genders: uir = a man.

mood   the grammatical form of a verb which shows whether it is in the indicative, subjunctive or imperative.

negative   expressing denial, refusal or prohibition. The words 'no' or 'not' are generally used.

neuter   one of the three genders: animal = an animal.

nominative　the case of the subject of a sentence or of the complement of a verb: *the king* is *angry* = rēx īrātus est.

noun　a word that names a person or thing: war = bellum.

numerals　numbers: in Latin these are either 'cardinals' (1, 2, 3, etc.), 'ordinals' (1st, 2nd, 3rd, etc.), 'distributives' (one each, two each, three each, etc.) or adverbs (once, twice, three times, etc.).

number　the state of being either singular or plural.

object　a noun or its equivalent acted upon by a transitive verb: the dog bit the boy: canis *puerum* momordit.

ordinals　see numerals.

part of speech　a grammatical term for the function of a word: noun, adjective, pronoun, verb, adverb, preposition, conjunction, interjection.

participle　an adjective formed from a verb. In Latin these are either present (a *loving* wife = uxor *amāns*), future (*about to love* her husband = uirum *amātūra*), and past (the *murdered* king = rēx *interfectus*).

passive　in the passive form the subject of the verb does not perform the action but experiences it: the king *was killed* = rēx *interfectus est*.

perfect tense　the tense of a verb that refers to a completed action. In English the word 'have' or 'has' is generally used: they *have lived* = uīxērunt.

person　a term that refers to the subject of a verb: 1st person - I (singular), we (plural); 2nd person — you (both singular and plural); 3rd person — he, she, it (singular), they (plural).

personal pronoun　a pronoun that refers to a person: e.g. I, you = ego, tū.

phrase　a distinct group of words which does not contain a finite verb: I swam *in the sea*.

pluperfect tense　the tense that means 'had', referring to an action already completed in the past: I *had* come to Rome = Rōmam aduēneram.

plural　of nouns, etc., referring to more than one: the trees = arborēs.

positive   not negative.

possessive pronoun   a pronoun that shows possession, belonging to someone or something: my, mine = meus, mea, meum.

prefix   a syllable or word added to the beginning of another word: *prōcēdō* = I *pro*ceed.

preposition   a word that stands in front of a noun or pronoun to produce an adverbial phrase. In Latin it will be followed by the accusative or ablative: *ante* merī-diem = *before* midday.

present tense   the tense of a verb that refers to something happening now: I am walking, I walk = ambulō.

principal parts   in Latin, the principal parts of active verbs generally consist of four elements, 1. the present tense, 2. the present infinitive, 3. the perfect tense, 4. the supine. Deponent and passive verbs do not have a supine.

pronoun   a word that stands instead of a noun or thing:e.g. he, she, this, that = is, ea, hoc, illud.

pronunciation   the way of pronouncing, or speaking, words.

reflexive pronoun   a word referring back to the subject of the verb, in which the action of the verb is performed on its subject: he washed *himself*: *sē* lāuit.

regular verb   a verb that follows a set pattern (i.e. that of one of the four conjugations) in its regular forms.

relative pronoun   a pronoun that introduces a subordinate clause, relating to the person or thing mentioned in the main clause: the man *who* loves me = uir *quī* mē amat.

sentence   a group of words, with a subject and a verb, that can stand on its own to make a statement, ask a question or give a command.

sequence of tenses   the process by which the use of a certain tense in the main clause determines the tense of the subjunctive used in a subordinate clause.

singular   of nouns, etc., referring to just one: the tree = arbor.

stem   the part of a noun or verb to which endings are added: *bell-* is the stem of *bell*um = war; *am-* is the stem of *am*ō = I love.

subject   in a clause or sentence, the noun or pronoun that causes the action of the verb: the *queen* killed the king = *rēgīna* rēgem interfēcit.

subjunctive   a verb form that is used, among many other functions, to express doubt or unlikelihood. Words such as *may*, *might*, *would*, *should* and *could* can indicate a subjunctive in English.

subordinate clause   a clause which depends on another clause (usually the main clause) of the sentence in which it stands. In the sentence 'This is a book which is hard to follow', 'which is hard to follow' describes the book. The clause would not make sense on its own. Thus it is subordinate.

superlative   the form of an adjective or adverb that makes it mean 'most' or 'very': *most* small (small*est*), *very* small = minimus.

supine   a part of the verb (the fourth of the principal parts) from which other forms of the verb, especially the passive, can be predicted.

syllable   part of a word that forms a spoken unit, usually a vowel sound with consonants before and/or after: mi-ni-mus.

tense   the form of a verb that shows when the action takes place: present, future, perfect, etc.

transitive verb   a verb used with a direct object either expressed or understood, e.g. *pick* apples or *pick till you are tired* (but not *he picked at the scab* — here 'picked' is intransitive).

verb   a word or group of words that describes an action: the children *had set* out = līberī *profectī erant*.

vocative   the case by which you address or call to someone: *Quintus*, come here = *Quīnte*, uenī hūc.

voice   the set of forms of a verb that show the relation of the subject to the action, i.e. active or passive.

vowel   a letter representing a vowel that can be spoken by itself: a, e, i, o, u, y.

Abbreviations

abl.	ablative
acc.	accusative
cf.	*cōnfer* (Latin for 'compare')
dat.	dative
e.g.	*exemplī grātiā* (Latin 'for the sake of an example', introducing an example)
etc.	*et cētera* (Latin for 'and so on')
f.	feminine
fem.	feminine
gen.	genitive
i.e.	*id est* (Latin for 'that is', introducing an explanation)
m.	masculine
masc.	masculine
n.	neuter
N.B.	*NOTĀ BENE* (Latin for 'note well')
nom.	nominative
p.	page
perf.	perfect
pl.	plural
pluperf.	pluperfect
plur.	plural
pp.	pages
sing.	singular
subj.	subjunctive

Pronunciation

Number of syllables and stress in Latin

The following rules should always be observed:

1 Except in obvious diphthongs (ae, au, oe, often eu), every single vowel signals a separate syllable, as in the English word recipe (three syllables). Thus in Latin **'dēsine'** is three syllables and **'diem'** is two.

2 The stress in Latin words of more than two syllables falls on the penultimate syllable if this is metrically 'heavy' (i.e. contains a 'long' vowel or a vowel before two consonants), e.g. **'festīnā'**, **'agénda'**. It falls on the antepenultimate (third from last) syllable when the penultimate syllable is metrically 'light' (i.e. contains a 'short' vowel before a single consonant), e.g. **'dóminus'**.

3 The stress almost always falls on the first syllable of two-syllable words.

4 What is recommended in **2** is natural for English speakers.

In this grammar (except where the material relates to English into Latin) all 'long' vowels are marked. Though a syllable containing any vowel before two consonants will probably be 'heavy' metrically, it does not follow that the vowel will be necessarily 'long'. All vowels which are unmarked, whether before two consonants or not, are 'short'.

☑ **Note:**

The distinction observed here between syllable *quantity* and vowel *length*, i.e. between (metrically) 'heavy' and 'light' syllables and (naturally) 'long' and 'short' vowels, is relatively recent. Older books use 'long' and 'short' indifferently for both syllables and vowels, thereby encouraging mispronunciation. The convention with regard to classical Latin assumes arbitrarily that a 'heavy' syllable takes twice as long to pronounce as a 'light' one.

The pronunciation of consonants and vowels

The English sounds referred to are those of standard southern British English.

1 | Consonants

Consonants are pronounced as in modern English, but note the following:

c   is always hard, as in **c**at (never soft as in ni**c**e). ····➤

g   is always hard, as in **G**od (except when it is followed by **n**; **gn** is sounded **ngn** as in ha**ngn**ail: so **magnus** is pronounced **mangnus**).

h   is always sounded, as in **h**ope.

i   is used as a consonant as well as a vowel; as a consonant it sounds like English **y**; so Latin **iam** is pronounced **yam**.

q   occurs, as in English, only before **u**; **qu** is sounded as in English **qu**ick.

r   is rolled as in Scots English, and is always sounded; so in Latin **sors** both **r** and **s** are sounded.

s   is always soft, as in **s**it (never like **z**, as in ro**s**e).

u   is used as a consonant as well as a vowel; it is pronounced like English **w**; so **uīdī** sounds **weedee**. There is no **v** in Latin.

Where double consonants occur, as in si**tt**ing, both consonants are pronounced; so **ille** is pronounced *ille* (l is sounded long as in English hall-light).

Distinguish between:

érās (you were)	and	**érrās** (you wander)
ádhūc (still)	and	**addúc** (lead to)
cátulus (puppy)	and	**Catúllus** (the name of a poet)

····➤ See the note on Church Latin at the end of the section on 'Diphthongs', p. 3.

2 | Vowels

a   short, as in English c**u**p (not as in c**a**p).

ā   long, as in English f**a**ther.

e   short, as in English p**e**t.

ē   long, as in English **ai**m (or, more accurately, French g**ai**).

i   short, as in English d**i**p.

ī   long, as in English d**ee**p.
o   short, as in English p**o**t.
ō   long, as in English m**o**bile (or, more accurately, French b**eau**).
u   short, as in English p**u**t.
ū   long, as in English f**oo**l.

3 | Diphthongs

A diphthong can be defined as a vowel (**a**, **e**, or **o**) followed by a glide
(**i**, **e** or **u**).

ae   as in English h**igh**. ····➤
au   as in English h**ow**.
ei   as in English **eigh**t.
eu   e-u (as in English t**e**ll, *not* as in English y**ew**).
oe   as in English b**oy** (only shorter).
ui   u-i (as in French **oui**).

····➤   In 'Church Latin' (the Latin used in the Roman Catholic Church), it is conventional
to pronounce sounds in an 'Italian' way; e.g. **c** and **g** before **e** and **i** are pronounced **ch**
and **j**, **gn** is pronounced **ny**, and **ae** is pronounced **ay**.

4 | One vowel followed by another separate vowel

In Latin words a vowel followed by another vowel (when the two vowels do
not form a diphthong) is almost invariably 'light' ('short'), e.g. **dĕus** (*god*),
galĕa (*helmet*), **tībĭa** (*pipe*). However, this does not necessarily apply in
Greek and, since many Greek proper names are used in Latin, I give a few
examples from many instances where the Latin rule of thumb would
mislead: ····➤

**Aenēās, Achelōus, Alphēus, Chrȳsēis, Cytherēa, Dēidamīa, Elegīa, Ĕ̄ous,
Īphigenīa, Lāodamīa, Menelāus, Thāis, Thalīa** (or **Thalēa**), **Trōicus**.

····➤   The above recommendations are based on W. Sidney Allen's *Vox Latina: A Guide to
the Pronunciation of Classical Latin* (Cambridge, 1965, revised 1978 & 1989).

However, over the centuries, Latin has sounded very different indeed from
what is recommended here. In the ancient world there were huge variations

over the vast expanse of the Roman Empire. And as Allen remarks, 'anyone who has listened to Latin as pronounced until recently in the Westminster play, or at Grace by elder members of Oxford and Cambridge high tables, or in legal phraseology, will be aware that it bears little relation to the pronunciation with which we have been concerned' (*Vox Latina*, p. 102).

Users of this grammar may therefore find it interesting to read the following brief account of the pronunciation of Latin in England, which is heavily indebted to Allen (*Vox Latina*, pp. 102–10); see also L. P. Wilkinson, *Golden Latin Artistry* (Cambridge, 1963), pp. 3–6).

The pronunciation of Latin in England

Throughout the centuries in which Latin has been spoken in England, native speech habits have had a considerable effect on the pronunciation of the language. In the Old English period there was no attempt to observe the correct vowel lengths except in the penultimate syllables of words of more than two syllables: thus **mínimīs** and **meliŏra**. The first syllable of a two-syllable word was rendered heavy by lengthening the first vowel if it was originally 'short' (e.g. **lībrum** for **librum**). Also s after vowels was pronounced as z.

After the Norman conquest, the French influence made itself strongly felt. Consonantal i and g (before vowels) were pronounced like j in **judge** (e.g. in **iūstum** and **genus**), c (before *i* or *e*) was pronounced like s (so **Cicerō** became **Siserō**, as he remains in English to this day), and long vowels before two or more consonants were pronounced short (**nūllus** becoming **nullus**). The tendency to lengthen short vowels was reinforced (e.g. **tēnet** and **fōcus** for **tenet** and **focus**).

In the mid-fourteenth century English started to establish itself as the medium for the teaching of Latin in England, which had its effect on the pronunciation of the language. Then in 1528 Erasmus's dialogue *De recta Latini Graecique sermonis prononciatione* (Concerning the correct pronunciation of Latin and Greek) was published in Basle. This light-hearted conversation between a bear (the instructor) and a lion was a milestone on the journey towards the re-establishment of the classical pronunciation. It recommends *inter alia* hard c and g before all vowels and the pronunciation of s as simply s where a z sound had become traditional (e.g. in **mīlitēs**). In addition it reasserts the importance of vowel length.

While Erasmus does not appear to have actually used his reformed pronunciation, his work had an important, if gradual, influence. Attempts to establish his recommended pronunciation at Cambridge, however, were temporarily halted when the Chancellor of the University published in 1542 an edict specifically forbidding it. Undergraduates, he claimed, were becoming insolent in making use of an exotic pronunciation and relishing the fact that their elders could not understand it.

The Chancellor's edict was repealed in 1558. Even so, the new pronunciation was obstructed by inertia and the prejudice of traditionalists as well as by developments in English as the Middle English vowel system shifted to that of modern English (the so-called Great English Vowel Shift). These meant that the Latin vowels a, i, and e (at least when stressed) were pronounced as in English *name*, *wine*, and *seen*. In addition, in words of more than two syllables with a light penultimate, the antepenultimate (stressed) vowel was generally shortened. Thus **Oedipus** and **Aeschylus** became **Edipus** and **Eschylus**—as they remain in the USA—and **Caesaris** became **Cesaris**.

In the mid-nineteenth century vowel length began to be correctly taught, and hard **g** and **c** were established in some quarters. However, around 1870 there came to a head a feeling that something far more radical had to be done about the chaos in the pronunciation of classical Latin, and by the end of the century all the responsible bodies in England representing schools, universities and learned societies had recommended the adoption of an authentic scheme of pronunciation formulated by various Cambridge and Oxford colleges.

However, inertia as well as downright opposition ensured that the reforms took at least a generation to come into effect. Especially controversial was the recognition that in Latin there is no sound **v** (the equivalent sound was English **w**). Thus what had been written **vēnī**, **vīdī**, **vīcī** should be pronounced *wayny*, *weedy*, *weaky*—which for some reason struck the reactionaries as being very funny.

Even as late as 1939 *The Times* received—and suppressed—a letter against the old pronunciation by the Kennedy Professor of Latin at Cambridge, and the controversy lingered on until the 1950s. Indeed, one elderly teacher at a famous English school could still be heard regularly using the old pronunciation in 1980. In addition, it has to be acknowledged that, as Allen crisply remarks, the reforms do not go so far as to involve any actually non-English sounds (*Vox Latina*, p. 106). In fact it has been Allen's work, enthusiastically propagated by the Joint Association of Classical Teachers, which has eventually shifted the English pronunciation of classical Latin closer to the Mediterranean basin.

Number, gender and cases

In English grammar we are familiar with the concept of *number*, i.e. singular and plural:

> The **boy was** attracted to the <u>girls</u> but <u>they were</u> not attracted to **him**.

Here the words in bold are singular while the words underlined are plural.

We are also familiar with the concept of *gender*, i.e. masculine, feminine, and neuter:

> The girl and the boy love the cat but it feels no affection for them.

Here the girl is 'feminine' and the boy is 'masculine'. While the cat will of course in reality be either male or female, it is here regarded as neither: hence the word 'it'. This is the 'neuter' gender.

Cases

Latin is an inflected language, i.e. the endings of most of its words change depending on their function in a sentence. English is largely uninflected, though some words do change according to their function:

> I looked for my father **whom** I had lost, but I could not find **him**.
> Meanwhile our mother was out looking for **us**.

'Whom', 'him', and 'us' are the *accusative* of 'who', 'he', and 'we'. (You can see how English tends to abolish inflection from the fact that most speakers nowadays would say 'who' and not 'whom' in this sentence.)

Verbs in tenses (see p. 32) are called finite verbs; they have *subjects* and often have *objects*. The subject carries out the action of the verb; the object is on the receiving end of the action of the verb. In the sentence above, 'I' is the subject of the verb 'looked for', 'my father' is its object. 'I' am doing the looking; he is being looked for. Which words are the subjects and the objects in the following sentences?

The gardener mowed the lawn.
The dog obstructed him.
I saw them.

The subject is in the *nominative* case, the object is in the *accusative*. In what cases are: *she, her, whom, he, them*?

Nominative and accusative are the names of just two of the Latin cases in Latin. In Latin there are seven of these cases and they have names which are almost all still used in English grammars (though in English the case we refer to below as the *ablative* tends to be called the 'instrumental' case). ····➤

In Latin the endings of nouns (note that there is no definite article (*the*) or indefinite article (*a* or *an*) in Latin), pronouns, and adjectives vary according to the case they are in.[1] In English this happens only in some pronouns, as in the examples above. The endings by which the cases are marked on most Latin nouns fall into a number of regular patterns. (The word 'case' comes from Latin **cadō** (I fall) and thus the word 'fall' is highly appropriate.) We call these patterns **declensions**. It is customary to recognize five of these. To *decline* is to go through the different cases of a noun, adjective or pronoun, in order.

In Latin, adjectives are in the same number, gender, and case as the nouns to which they refer. (This is called *agreement*.) The endings, however, could well be different, since the adjective may belong to a different declension from its noun.

····➤ 1 In the vocabulary lists in this Grammar, nouns are given in their nominative and genitive singular, and adjectives are given in their nominative singular, masculine, feminine, and neuter.

---

1 | Nominative

The nominative is, as we have seen, the case of the *subject* of the verb:

Quīntus ambulābat.
Quintus was walking.

It is also used of the *complement* of the verb:

Quīntus est *frāter meus*.
Quintus is my brother.

2 | Genitive

The basic meaning of the genitive case is 'of'. It is used mainly in these senses:

- possessive:
  uīllam *mātris meae* uendidī.
  I sold my mother's villa (the villa of my mother).

- partitive:
  fer mihi plūs uīnī.
  Bring me more wine (literally, more of wine).

- descriptive (this is often called the genitive of quality):
  fēmina *magnae prūdentiae*
  a woman of great good sense

- characterizing:
  ***bonī* est rēm pūblicam cōnseruāre.**
  It is characteristic of a good man to look after the state.

- of value:
  ōrātiō *nūllīus mōmentī*
  a speech of no importance

- after the verbs of remembering and forgetting (both can also take an accusative)

meminī, meminisse	I remember
oblīuīscor, oblīuīscī, oblītus sum	I forget

- expressing the charge after the verbs:

absoluō, absoluere, absoluī, absolūtum	I acquit
accūsō (1)	I accuse
damnō, condemnō (1)	I condemn

  ***māiestātis* Petrōnium accūsō.**
  I accuse Petronius *of* treason.

  ***sīcārium illum capitis damnō.*[1] ····➤**
  I condemn that assassin to death.

····➤ 1. In this example 'caput', meaning head or life, is the penalty.

- after the following adjectives:

auidus, auida, auidum	greedy (for)
cōnscius, cōnscia, cōnscium	conscious (of)
cupidus, cupida, cupidum	desirous (of)
expers, expers, expers	without, lacking

memor, memor, memor	mindful (of), remembering
immemor, immemor, immemor	unmindful (of), forgetting
nescius, nescia, nescium	not knowing, ignorant (of)
perītus, perīta, perītum	expert (in), experienced (in)
plēnus, plēna, plēnum ····➤	full (of)[2]
studiōsus, studiōsa, studiōsum	eager (for)
similis, similis, simile ····➤	like[3]
dissimilis, dissimilis, dissimile	unlike[3]
fīlius *patris* simillimus	a son very like his father

····➤ 2. This adjective can also be used with the ablative.
····➤ 3. A genitive is always correct after these; a dative can also be used.

● in front of the 'postpositions' **causā** and **grātiā**, both meaning 'for the sake of'. Postpositions are prepositions which follow the noun dependent on them.

> ***uestrae salūtis* grātiā**
> for the sake of your safety

3 | Dative

The basic meanings of the dative case are 'to' and 'for'. It goes naturally with verbs of giving (it derives from the Latin word **dō** (I give): **datum** means 'given'). These verbs are regularly followed by a direct object in the accusative and an indirect object in the dative:

> **librum *fīliae meae* dedī.**
> I gave a book (direct object) ***to*** my daughter (indirect object)—*or*
> I gave my daughter a book.

Other uses of the dative include:

● possessive:
> **est *mihi* canis.**
> I have a dog (literally, there is to me a dog).

● of advantage or disadvantage:
> **rem pūblicam *nōbīs* seruāuit.**
> He saved the state for us.

- of separation:
  gladium *mihi* rapuit.
  He snatched my sword from me.[1]····▸
- the so-called 'ethic' or 'polite' dative:
  aperī *mihi* hanc iānuam.
  Open this door for me, i.e. Please open this door.[2]····▸
- after a large number of verbs (see pp. 11–12).

····▸ 1. This is in fact a dative of disadvantage.
····▸ 2. Compare in Elizabethan English 'Knock me this door'.

| Verbs followed by the dative case

appropinquō(1)	I approach
cōnfīdō, cōnfīdere, cōnfīsus sum	I trust, have confidence in
diffīdō, diffīdere, diffīsus sum	I mistrust
cōnsulō[3]**, cōnsulere, cōnsuluī, cōnsultum**····▸	I take care of, provide for[3]
crēdō, crēdere, crēdidī, crēditum	I believe, trust
faueō, fauēre, fāuī, fautum	I favour, back up
grātulor(1)	I congratulate
ignōscō, ignōscere, ignōuī, ignōtum	I forgive, pardon (like **nōscō**)
immineō, imminēre, —, —	I threaten, overhang
indulgeō, indulgēre, indulsī, indulsum	I am kind to, am lenient to
inuideō, inuidēre, inuīdī, inuīsum	I envy, grudge (like **uideō**)
īrāscor, īrāscī, īrātus sum	I am angry (with)
medeor(2)	I heal
noceō(2)	I hurt
nūbō, nūbere, nūpsī, nūptum	I marry (woman as subject)
obstō, obstāre, obstitī, obstitum	I stand in the way of, withstand, hinder (like **stō**, but note **obstitī, obstitum**)
occurrō, occurrere, occurrī, occursum	I run to meet (like **currō**)
succurrō, succurrere, succurrī, succursum	I run to help
parcō, parcere, pepercī, parsum	I spare

····▸ 3. When **cōnsulō** is followed by the accusative, it means '*I consult*'

pāreō (2)	I obey
persuādeō, persuādēre, persuāsī, persuāsum	I persuade
placeō (2)	I please
displiceō (2)	I displease
praecipiō, praecipere, praecēpī, praeceptum	I teach, order (like **capiō**, but note **praeceptum**)
resistō, resistere, restitī, —	I resist
seruiō (4)	I am a slave to, work for
studeō, studēre, studuī, —	I devote myself to, am keen on, study
subueniō, subuenīre, subuēnī, subuentum	I come to the help of (like **ueniō**)

 Note:

Most of these verbs fall into the categories of

either	helping, favouring, obeying, pleasing, serving
or	ordering, persuading, trusting, sparing, pardoning, envying, being angry.

Note also these verbs followed by the accusative and the dative:

tibi aliquid obiciō, obicere, obiēcī, obiectum.
I throw something in your way.
(I reproach you with something.)

tē exercituī praeficiō.
I put you in charge of the army.

Compounds of **sum** (except for **possum, absum, īnsum**) are followed by the dative:

senātuī adsum.	I am present at the senate.
gemmae dēsunt mihi.	I lack jewels.
hīs rēbus interfuī.	I was involved in these things.
exercituī praesum.	I am in command of the army.
cōnsilium tuum mihi prōdest.	Your advice is useful to me (benefits me).
parentibus superfuī.	I survived my parents.

The predicative dative is frequently used with the verb 'to be', as in the following expressions:

argumentō esse	to be proof
auxiliō esse	to be a means of help
bonō esse	to profit, be advantageous
cordī esse	to be dear
cūrae esse	to be a cause of concern
damnō esse	to hurt, harm
dēdecorī esse	to be a cause of shame
dētrīmentō esse	to be harmful, to cause loss
dolōrī esse	to be a cause of grief
dōnō esse	as a present
exemplō esse	to be an example
exitiō esse	to prove the destruction (of)
honōrī esse	to be an honour
impedīmentō esse	to be a hindrance
lucrō esse	to be profitable
lūdibriō esse	to be an object of ridicule
malō esse	to harm
odiō esse	to be an object of hatred
onerī esse	to be a burden
praesidiō esse	to be a defence, a protection
pudōrī esse	to be a cause of shame
salūtī esse	to prove the salvation (of)
subsidiō esse	to be a help
ūsuī esse	to be of use, benefit

Horatius, quia tam fortis erat, nōn modo suīs *magnō praesidiō* fuit sed etiam reī pūblicae *salūtī.*

Because he was so brave, Horatius proved not only a strong defence to his men but also the salvation of the state.

For the dative of the agent with the gerundive, see p. 111.

4 | Accusative

The accusative is, as we have seen, the case of the *object*:

cauē *canem*!

Beware of the dog!

- It is also used after a large number of prepositions (see pp. 29–30).
- It is used in expressions of time, place, and space (see pp. 71–5).

- Exclamations are in the accusative:

mē miserum!
poor me!
ō tempora! ō mōrēs!
o these times! o these customs! (i.e. what have things come to!)

- The subject of the infinitive is in the accusative:

sapientem eum esse crēdō.
I believe him to be wise.

5 | Ablative

The basic meanings of the ablative case are 'by', 'with', 'from', 'at', 'in' or 'on'. When the meaning is 'by' and it is a living creature that performs the action, Latin uses *ā* or *ab* with the ablative:

rēgīna *ā marītō suō* occīsa est.
The queen was killed by her own husband.

When the action is caused by an inanimate object, Latin uses the ablative without *ā* or *ab*:

canis *lapide* laesus est.
The dog was injured by a stone.

The ablative is also used after a large number of prepositions (see pp. 29–30). It is used in expressions of time, place, and space (see pp. 71–5).

- Note the ablative of description:

puer *longīs capillīs*
a boy with long hair

puella *maximā prūdentiā*
a girl of the greatest good sense

Unlike the genitive of description (see p. 8), it can be used of visible and tangible qualities, as in the first example above. This usage is often called the ablative of quality.

- the ablative of price:

uīllam *magnō pretiō* ēmī.
I bought the villa at a considerable price.

Compare the genitive of value:

hanc uīllam maximī aestimō.
I value this house very highly.

Note the following ablatives of price:

magnō	at a great price
plūrimō	at a very great price
paruō	at a small (low) price
nihilō	for nothing
uīlī	cheaply

● The ablative of comparison. When *quam* (than) is not used, the object of comparison (i.e. the word after 'than' in English) is in the ablative:

sorōre meā sapientior sum.
I am cleverer than my sister.

But note that in classical prose *quam* is the norm for this kind of comparison. The ablative of comparison came to be used as an alternative in the poets particularly.

● The ablative of the measure of difference:

soror mea sorōre tuā *multō* sapientior est.
My sister is much wiser (*literally*, wiser by much) than yours.

● For the ablative absolute construction, see pp. 79–80.

The following verbs are followed by the ablative:

abūtor, abūtī, abūsus sum	I use up, waste, misuse
careō (2)	I am without, lack
egeō (2)	I am without, lack
fruor, fruī, frūctus (or **fruitus**) **sum**	I enjoy
fungor, fungī, fūnctus sum	I perform, discharge (sometimes with acc.)
opus est mihi (**tibi**, etc.)	I (you, etc.) need
gladiō puellae opus est.	
The girl needs a sword.	
potior (4)	I take possession of, possess[1] ····▶
uēscor, uēscī, —	I feed on
ūtor, ūtī, ūsus sum	I use

····▶ 1. **potior** can also be followed by the accusative and genitive.

● The ablative is used after the following adjectives:

contentus, contenta, contentum	contented with, satisfied with
dignus, digna, dignum	worthy of
indignus, indigna, indignum	unworthy of

frētus, frēta, frētum	relying on
orbus, orba, orbum	deprived of, bereft of
praeditus, praedita, praeditum	endowed with

6 | Vocative

The vocative is the case by which you address or call to someone:

Quīnte, **cauē canem!**
Quintus, beware of the dog!

The vocative is in most instances indistinguishable in form from the nominative in Latin, and we have therefore omitted it from our tables of grammar. We have referred in a note to the kinds of word in which it is different.

7 | Locative

The locative case tells us the place where something is happening:

Rōmae	at Rome
domī	at home
rūrī	in the country
humī	on the ground

See note 8 on p. 18.

| Practice sentences

Translate into English or Latin as appropriate:

1 **Brūtus Cassiusque Caesarem dictātōrem occīdērunt.**
2 **uir magnae auctōritātis—homō nihilī—animō ignāuus, procāx ōre.**
3 **plūs praedae mīlitibus dōnat.**
4 **bēstiae sunt ratiōnis et ōrātiōnis expertēs.** (Cicero, de officiis, 1.51)
5 **cīuis bonī est lēgibus pārēre.**
6 **perfer et obdūrā: multō grauiōra tulistī.** (Ovid, Tristia, 5.11.7)
7 Romulus founded the city (of) Rome.
8 His deeds were a cause of shame to the Greeks.
9 One man is in command of all the Romans.
10 The horse was worth a lot of money but I bought it cheaply.
11 She is much more stupid than her brother.
12 I forgot his words, but my friend remembered them.

Reference Grammar

Nouns

	1st declension	2nd declension	
	stems in -a	stems in -o	
	feminine	masculine	neuter
singular			
nom.	puell-a (*girl*)	domin-us (*master*)	bell-um (*war*)
gen.	puell-ae	domin-ī	bell-ī
dat.	puell-ae	domin-ō	bell-ō
acc.	puell-am	domin-um	bell-um
abl.	puell-ā	domin-ō	bell-ō
plural			
nom.	puell-ae	domin-ī	bell-a
gen.	puell-ārum	domin-ōrum	bell-ōrum
dat.	puell-īs	domin-īs	bell-īs
acc.	puell-ās	domin-ōs	bell-a
abl.	puell-īs	domin-īs	bell-īs

	3rd declension			
	stems in consonants		stems in i	
	masc. & fem.	neuter	masc. & fem.	neuter
singular				
nom.	rēx (*king*, m.)	lītus (*shore*)	nāuis (*ship*, f.)	mare (*sea*)
gen.	rēg-is	lītor-is	nāu-is	mar-is
dat.	rēg-ī	lītor-ī	nāu-ī	mar-ī
acc.	rēg-em	lītus	nāu-em	mare
abl.	rēg-e	lītor-e	nāu-e	mar-ī
plural				
nom.	rēg-ēs	lītor-a	nāu-ēs	mar-ia
gen.	rēg-um	lītor-um	nāu-ium	mar-ium
dat.	rēg-ibus	lītor-ibus	nāu-ibus	mar-ibus
acc.	rēg-ēs	lītor-a	nāu-ēs (-īs)	mar-ia
abl.	rēg-ibus	lītor-ibus	nāu-ibus	mar-ibus

3rd declension

	ending in 2 consonants	stems in-r (or-l)
	masc. & fem.	**masc. & fem.**
singular		
nom.	urbs (*city*, f.)	pater (*father*, m.)
gen.	urb-is	patr-is
dat.	urb-ī	patr-ī
acc.	urb-em	patr-em
abl.	urb-e	patr-e
plural		
nom.	urb-ēs	patr-ēs
gen.	urb-ium	patr-um
dat.	urb-ibus	patr-ibus
acc.	urb-ēs (-īs)	patr-ēs
abl.	urb-ibus	patr-ībus

4th declension / 5th declension

	stems in -u		stems in -e
	masc.	**neuter**	**feminine**
singular			
nom.	grad-us (*step*)	corn-ū (*horn, wing*	r-ēs (*thing*)
gen.	grad-ūs	corn-ūs *of an army*)	r-eī
dat.	grad-uī	corn-uī	r-eī
acc.	grad-um	corn-ū	r-em
abl.	grad-ū	corn-ū	r-ē
plural			
nom.	grad-ūs	corn-ua	r-ēs
gen.	grad-uum	corn-uum	r-ērum
dat.	grad-ibus	corn-ibus	r-ēbus
acc.	grad-ūs	corn-ua	r-ēs
abl.	grad-ibus	corn-ibus	r-ēbus

••••➤ Notes

1   The vocative is the same as the nominative for all nouns of all declensions except for 2nd declension masculine nouns in **-us**, e.g. **domin-us**, which form vocative singular **-e**, e.g. **domin-e**; and in **-ius**, e.g. **fīl-ius** (son), which form vocative singular **-ī**, e.g. **fīl-ī**.

2   All nouns of the 1st declension are feminine except for a few which are masculine by meaning, e.g. **nauta** (sailor), **agricola** (farmer), **scrība** (clerk, secretary).

3 2nd declension masculine nouns with nominative singular **-er**, e.g. **puer** (boy), **ager** (field): some keep **-e-** in the other cases, e.g. **puer, puer-ī**; others drop it, e.g. **ager, agr-ī**.

The genitive singular of masculine nouns ending **-ius** and neuter nouns ending **-ium** in nominative is often contracted from **-iī** to **-ī**, e.g. **fīlī** (son), **ingenī** (character).

4 The following 2nd declension nouns have minor irregularities: **deus** (god) has nominative plural **deī** or **dī**, genitive plural **deōrum** or **deum**, ablative plural **deīs** or **dīs**; **uir, uirī** (man) has genitive plural **uirōrum** or **uirum**.

5 3rd declension. The gender of all 3rd declension nouns has to be learned.

Genitive plural: the general rule is that nouns with stems in **i** have genitive plural **-ium**, while those with stems in consonants have genitive plural **-um**. All nouns with nominative **-is**, e.g. **nāuis**, have stems in **i**. And so do nouns with nominatives that end in two consonants, e.g. **fōns** (spring), **urbs**, genitive plural **fontium, urbium** (their original nominative was, e.g., **urbis**). Apart from these nouns ending in two consonants, if a 3rd declension noun gets longer in the genitive singular, it does not get any longer in the genitive plural (which therefore ends in **-um**); and if it does not get longer in the genitive singular, its genitive plural ends in **-ium** (exceptions: **canis** (dog), **iuuenis** (young man), **senex** (old man), **sēdēs** (seat, residence), **pater** (father), **māter** (mother), **frāter** (brother)).

Nouns with stems in **ī** have alternative forms for ablative singular, e.g. **nāue** or **nāuī**, and for accusative plural, e.g. **nāuēs** or **nāuīs**. But **uīs** (force) in singular has only accusative **uim** and ablative **uī**. The plural **uīrēs** (strength) is regular, with genitive **uīrium**.

6 Most 4th declension nouns are masculine; **manus** (hand) is feminine, as is **domus** (house, home), which has alternative 2nd declension endings in the dative singular (**domuī** or **domō**) and in the genitive and accusative plural (**domuum** or **domōrum**, **domūs** or **domōs**); locative **domī**.

There are very few neuter 4th declension nouns; the only common ones are **cornū** and **genū** (knee).

7 All 5th declension nouns are feminine except for **diēs** (day), which can be masculine or feminine.

8 The locative case, meaning where:

1st declension singular: **-ae**, e.g. **Rōmae** (at Rome)
plural: **-īs**, e.g. **Athēnīs** (at Athens)

2nd declension singular: **-ī**, e.g. **Corinthī** (at Corinth)
plural: **-īs**, e.g. **Philippīs** (at Philippi)

3rd declension singular: **-ī/e**, e.g. **rūrī, rūre** (in the country), **humī** (on the ground)
plural: **-ibus**, e.g. **Gādibus** (at Cadiz).

| Adjectives

Masculine & neuter 2nd declension; feminine 1st declension

singular	m.	f.	n.
nom.	bon-us (*good*)	bon-a	bon-um
gen.	bon-ī	bon-ae	bon-ī
dat.	bon-ō	bon-ae	bon-ō
acc.	bon-um	bon-am	bon-um
abl.	bon-ō	bon-ā	bon-ō

plural			
nom.	bon-ī	bon-ae	bon-a
gen.	bon-ōrum	bon-ārum	bon-ōrum
dat.	bon-īs	bon-īs	bon-īs
acc.	bon-ōs	bon-ās	bon-a
abl.	bon-īs	bon-īs	bon-īs

••••▶ Note

Similarly, **miser** (wretched), **misera**, **miserum** (keeping **-e-** like **puer**) and **pulcher** (beautiful), **pulchra**, **pulchrum** (dropping the **-e-**, like **ager**).

3rd declension

	consonant stems		stems in -ri	
singular	m. & f.	n.	m. & f.	n.
nom.	pauper (*poor*)	pauper	ācer (*keen*)[1]	ācr-e
gen.	pauper-is	pauper-is	ācr-is	ācr-is
dat.	pauper-ī	pauper-ī	ācr-ī	ācr-ī
acc.	pauper-em	pauper	ācr-em	ācr-e
abl.	pauper-e	pauper-e	ācr-ī	ācr-ī

plural				
nom.	pauper-ēs	pauper-a	ācr-ēs	ācr-ia
gen.	pauper-um	pauper-um	ācr-ium	ācr-ium
dat.	pauper-ibus	pauper-ibus	ācr-ibus	ācr-ibus
acc.	pauper-ēs	pauper-a	ācr-ēs	ācr-ia
abl.	pauper-ibus	pauper-ibus	ācr-ibus	ācr-ibus

••••▶ 1. But **f.** ācr-is; ācr-is; ācr-ī; etc.

3rd declension

stems in **i**

singular	m. & f.	n.
nom.	omnis (all)	omn-e
gen.	omn-is	omn-is
dat.	omn-ī	omn-ī
acc.	omn-em	omn-e
abl.	omn-ī	omn-ī

plural		
nom.	omn-ēs	omn-ia
gen.	omn-ium	omn-ium
dat.	omn-ibus	omn-ibus
acc.	omn-ēs (-īs)	omn-ia
abl.	omn-ibus	omn-ibus

stems in **i**

singular	m. & f.	n.
nom.	ingēns (huge)	ingēns
gen.	ingent-is	ingent-is
dat.	ingent-ī	ingent-ī
acc.	ingent-em	ingēns
abl.	ingent-ī	ingent-ī

plural		
nom.	ingent-ēs	ingent-ia
gen.	ingent-ium	ingent-ium
dat.	ingent-ibus	ingent-ibus
acc.	ingent-ēs (-īs)	ingent-ia
abl.	ingent-ibus	ingent-ibus

••••▶ Notes

1 Most 3rd declension adjectives have stems in **i**. Other types of adjective with stems in **i** are: **ferōx** (fierce; neuter **ferōx**), genitive **ferōc-is**; **celer** (quick; feminine **celeris**, neuter **celere**), genitive **celer-is**.

2 3rd declension adjectives with stems in consonants are few, e.g. **dīues** (rich), **dīuit-is**; **pauper**, **pauper-is**; **uetus** (old), **ueter-is**; and the comparative adjective, e.g. **fortior** (stronger, braver; neuter **fortius**), genitive **fortiōr-is**.

3 While the ablative of **ingēns** is **ingentī**, present participles, e.g. **amāns** (loving), end their ablatives in **-e** (**amante**) when used not as adjectives, but as participles.

Mixed 2nd and 3rd declensions

	alter (*one* or *the other of two*)			uter (*which of two?*)		
singular	**m.**	**f.**	**n.**	**m.**	**f.**	**n.**
nom.	alter	altera	alterum	uter	utra	utrum
gen.	alterĭus	alterĭus	alterĭus	utrĭus	utrĭus	utrĭus
dat.	alterī	alterī	alterī	utrī	utrī	utrī
acc.	alterum	alteram	alterum	utrum	utram	utrum
abl.	alterō	alterā	alterō	utrō	utrā	utrō

Plural like that of **bon-ī, bon-ae, bon-a**. Similarly: **uterque, utraque, utrumque**
(*each of two*).

The following adjectives have the same characteristics, i.e. gen. sing. **-ĭus**,
dat. sing. **-ī**:

alius, alia, aliud	**other**	gen. sing.	[alĭus]	dat. sing	aliī
nūllus, nūlla, nūllum	**no**		nūllĭus		nūllī
ūllus, ūlla, ūllum	**any**		ūllĭus		ūllī
sōlus, sōla, sōlum	**only**		sōlĭus		sōlī
tōtus, tōta, tōtum	**whole**		tōtĭus		tōtī
ūnus, ūna, ūnum	**one**		ūnĭus		ūnī

····▶ Note
nēmō (*no one*) which declines: **nēmō, nēminem, nūllĭus, nēminī, nūllō.**

| Comparison of adjectives

Most adjectives add **-ior** to the stem to form the comparative and **-issimus** to
form the superlative:

positive	comparative	superlative
longus	**longior**	**longissimus**
long	longer, further	longest, very long
trīstis	**trīstior**	**trīstissimus**
sad	sadder	saddest, very sad

····▶ Note
1 The comparative can mean 'quite', 'rather', or 'too', e.g. **trīstior** can mean not only
   'sadder' but 'quite sad', 'rather sad', or 'too sad'.

2 **quam** followed by the superlative means 'as ... possible', e.g. **quam longissimus**
   means 'as long as possible'.

The comparative declines as a 3rd declension adjective (consonant stem):

| | singular | | plural | |
	m. & f.	n.	m. & f.	n.
nom.	longior	longius	longiōrēs	longiōra
gen.	longiōris	longiōris	longiōrum	longiōrum
dat.	longiōrī	longiōrī	longiōribus	longiōribus
acc.	longiōrem	longius	longiōrēs	longiōra
abl.	longiōre	longiōre	longiōribus	longiōribus

The superlative declines like **bonus, bona, bonum**.

The following common adjectives have irregular comparison:

positive	comparative	superlative
bonus (*good*)	melior	optimus
malus (*bad*)	peior	pessimus
magnus (*great*)	maior	maximus
multus (*much*)	plūs*	plūrimus
paruus (*small*)	minor	minimus
senex (*old*)	nātū maior	nātū maximus
iuuenis (*young*)	nātū minor	nātū minimus
	iūnior	

* **plūs** in the singular is a neuter noun, declining: **plūs, plūris, plūrī, plūs, plūre**. So **plūs cibī** = more (of) food. In the plural it is an adjective: **plūrēs, plūra**, etc. So **plūrēs puellae** = more girls.

Adjectives ending **-er** in the nominative double the **-r-** in the superlative, e.g.

miser, (wretched) **miserior, miserrimus**

pulcher, (beautiful) **pulchrior, pulcherrimus**

celer, (quick) **celerior, celerrimus**

Six adjectives with nominative **-ilis** double the **-l-** in the superlative:

facilis (easy)**, facilior, facillimus**

difficilis (difficult)**, difficilior, difficillimus**

gracilis (slender)**, gracilior, gracillimus**

humilis (low)**, humilior, humillimus**

similis (like)**, similior, simillimus**

dissimilis (unlike)**, dissimilior, dissimillimus**

Other adjectives with nominative **-ilis** form regular superlatives,
e.g. **amābilis** (loveable), **amābilior, amābilissimus**.

| Adverbs

1 From **bonus** type adjectives, adverbs are usually formed by adding -**ē** to the
stem, e.g. **lent-us** (slow): **lent-ē** (slowly); **miser** (wretched): **miser-ē**
(wretchedly). A few add -**ō**, e.g. **subit-us** (sudden): **subit-ō** (suddenly).

2 From 3rd declension adjectives, adverbs are usually formed by adding
-**ter** to the stem. e.g. **fēlīx** (fortunate): **fēlīci-ter** (fortunately); **celer** (quick):
celeri-ter (quickly). A few 3rd declension adjectives use the accusative
neuter singular as an adverb, e.g. **facilis** (easy), **facile** (easily); so also
comparative adverbs. e.g. **fortior** (braver), **fortius** (more bravely).

3 There are many adverbs which have no corresponding adjectival form,
e.g. **diū** (for a long time), **quandō** (when?), **iam** (now, already), **semper**
(always).

4 **Comparison of adverbs.** The comparative adverb is the same as the neuter
accusative of the comparative adjective; the superlative adverb is formed by
changing the nominative ending **-us** to **-ē**, e.g.

adjective	adverb	comparative adverb	superlative adverb
longus (*long*)	longē (far)	longius	longissimē
fortis (*strong, brave*)	fortiter	fortius	fortissimē

Note the following irregular adverbs:

adjective	adverb	comparative adverb	superlative adverb
bonus (*good*)	bene	melius	optimē
malus (*bad*)	male	peius	pessimē
facilis (*easy*)	facile	facilius	facillimē
magnus (*great*)	magnopere	magis (*more*, of degree)	maximē (*most, very greatly*)
multus (*much*)	multum	plūs (*more*, of quantity)	plūrimum (*most, very much*)
paruus (*small*)	paul(l)um	minus	minimē
prīmus (*first*)	prīmum	—	—
	diū (*for a long time*)	diūtius	diūtissimē
	post (*after*)	posterius	postrēmō

(irregular adverbs *cont.*)

adjective	adverb	comparative adverb	superlative adverb
	prope (*near*)	propius	proximē
	saepe (*often*)	saepius	saepissimē
		potius (*rather*)	potissimum (*especially*)

Numerals

cardinals

1 ūnus I		**16** sēdecim XVI	
2 duo II		**17** septendecim XVII	
3 trēs III		**18** duodēuīgintī XVIII	
4 quattuor IV		**19** ūndēuīgintī XIX	
5 quīnque V		**20** uīgintī XX	
6 sex VI		**30** trīgintā XXX	
7 septem VII		**40** quadrāgintā XL	
8 octō VIII		**50** quīnquāgintā L	
9 novem IX		**100** centum C	
10 decem X		**200** ducentī, -ae, -a CC	
11 ūndecim XI		**300** trecentī, -ae, -a CCC	
12 duodecim XII		**400** quadringentī, -ae, -a CCCC	
13 tredecim XIII		**500** quīngentī D	
14 quattuordecim XIV		**1,000** mīlle M	
15 quīndecim XV		**2,000** duo mīlia MM	

····▶ **Notes**

1 The numbers 4–100 do not decline; 200–900 decline like **bonī, -ae, -a**.

2 Compound numbers: 24, for example, is **uīgintī quattuor** or **quattuor et uīgintī** (cf. English 'four and twenty').

3 **mīlle** does not decline; **mīlia** is a 3rd declension noun, so:
mīlle passūs = a mile (1,000 paces)
duo mīlia passuum = 2 miles (2,000 (of) paces).

4 Adverbial numbers: **semel, bis, ter, quater, quīnquiēns, sexiēns, septiēns, octiēns, nouiēns, deciēns** (once, twice, three times etc.); **centiēns** (100 times); **mīliēns** (1,000 times). The ending **-iēns** is often found as **-iēs**.

ordinals

1st	prīmus, -a, -um	**14th**	quārtus, -a, -um decimus, -a, -um etc.
2nd	secundus, -a, -um/alter, -a, -um		
3rd	tertius, -a, -um	**19th**	duodēuīcēnsimus, -a, -um
4th	quārtus, -a, -um	**20th**	uīcēnsimus, -a, -um
5th	quīntus, -a, -um	**30th**	trīcēnsimus, -a, -um
6th	sextus, -a, -um	**40th**	quadrāgēnsimus, -a, -um
7th	septimus, -a, -um	**50th**	quīnquāgēnsimus, -a, -um
8th	octāvus, -a, -um	**60th**	sexāgēnsimus, -a, -um
9th	nōnus, -a, -um	**70th**	septuāgēnsimus, -a, -um
10th	decimus, -a, -um	**80th**	octōgēnsimus, -a, -um
11th	ūndecimus, -a, -um	**90th**	nōnāgēnsimus, -a, -um
12th	duodecimus, -a, -um	**100th**	centēnsimus, -a, -um
13th	tertius, -a, -um decimus, -a, -um	**1,000th**	mīllēnsimus, -a, -um

••••▶ **Note**

The ending **-ēnsimus** is often found as **-ēsimus**.

Declension of ūnus, duo, trēs

	m.	f.	n.
nom.	ūnus (one)	ūna	ūnum
gen.	ūnĭus	ūnĭus	ūnĭus
dat.	ūnī	ūnī	ūnī
acc.	ūnum	ūnam	ūnum
abl.	ūnō	ūnā	ūnō

	m.	f.	n.
nom.	duo (two)	duae	duo
gen.	duōrum	duārum	duōrum
dat.	duōbus	duābus	duōbus
acc.	duōs	duās	duo
abl.	duōbus	duābus	duōbus

	m.	f.	n.
nom.	trēs (three)	trēs	tria
gen.	trium	trium	trium
dat.	tribus	tribus	tribus
acc.	trēs	trēs	tria
abl.	tribus	tribus	tribus

| Pronouns

personal pronouns

singular

nom.	ego(*I*)	tū (*you*)	
gen.	meī	tuī	suī (*himself, herself*)
dat.	mihĭ	tibĭ	sibĭ
acc.	mē	tē	sē
abl.	mē	tē	sē

plural

nom.	nōs (*we*)	uōs (*you*)	
gen.	nostrum, nostrī	uestrum, uestrī	suī (*themselves*)
dat.	nōbīs	uōbīs	sibi
acc.	nōs	uōs	sē
abl.	nōbīs	uōbīs	sē

••••▶ Notes

1 Note the way the ablative of these words combines with **cum** (with): **mēcum** (with me), **nōbīscum** (with us), etc.

2 The genitives **nostrī** and **uestrī** are objective, e.g. **cupidus nostrī** (desirous of us, wanting us); the genitives **nostrum** and **uestrum** are partitive, e.g. **ūnus uestrum** (one of you).

Possessive adjectives:

> meus, -a, -um (*my*)*
> tuus, -a, -um (*your*)
> suus, -a, -um (*his own, her own*)
> noster, nostra, nostrum (*our*)
> uester, uestra, uestrum (*your*)
> suus, -a, -um (*their own*)

*All decline like **bonus**, **-a**, **-um** or **pulcher**, **pulchr-a**, **pulchr-um** but the vocative of **meus** is **mī**

deictic pronouns

singular

	m.	f.	n.	m.	f.	n.
nom.	hic (*this*)	haec	hoc	ille (*that*)	illa	illud
gen.	huius	huius	huius	illĭus	illĭus	illĭus
dat.	huic	huic	huic	illī	illī	illī
acc.	hunc	hanc	hoc	illum	illam	illud
abl.	hōc	hāc	hōc	illō	illā	illō

	m.	f.	n.	m.	f.	n.
plural						
nom.	hī	hae	haec	illī	illae	illa
gen.	hōrum	hārum	hōrum	illōrum	illārum	illōrum
dat.	hīs	hīs	hīs	illīs	illīs	illīs
acc.	hōs	hās	haec	illōs	illās	illa
abl.	hīs	hīs	hīs	illīs	illīs	illīs
singular						
nom.	is*	ea	id	ipse (*self*)	ipsa	ipsum
gen.	eius	eius	eius	ipsĭus	ipsĭus	ipsĭus
dat.	eī	eī	eī	ipsī	ipsī	ipsī
acc.	eum	eam	id	ipsum	ipsam	ipsum
abl.	eō	eā	eō	ipsō	ipsā	ipsō

* (*he, she, it: that*)

	m.	f.	n.	m.	f.	n.
plural						
nom.	eī	eae	ea	ipsī	ipsae	ipsa
gen.	eōrum	eārum	eōrum	ipsōrum	ipsārum	ipsōrum
dat.	eīs	eīs	eīs	ipsīs	ipsīs	ipsīs
acc.	eōs	eās	ea	ipsōs	ipsās	ipsa
abl.	eīs	eīs	eīs	ipsīs	ipsīs	ipsīs

singular			
nom.	īdem (*same*)	eadem	idem
gen.	eiusdem	eiusdem	eiusdem
dat.	eīdem	eīdem	eīdem
acc.	eundem	eandem	idem
abl.	eōdem	eādem	eōdem

plural			
nom.	(e)īdem	eaedem	eadem
gen.	eōrundem	eārundem	eōrundem
dat.	eīsdem	eīsdem	eīsdem
acc.	eōsdem	eāsdem	eadem
abl.	eīsdem	eīsdem	eīsdem

relative pronoun

	m.	f.	n.
singular			
nom.	quī (*who,*	quae	quod
gen.	cuius *which*)	cuius	cuius
dat.	cui	cui	cui
acc.	quem	quam	quod
abl.	quō	quā	quō

Pronouns (continued)

plural	m.	f.	n.
nom.	quī	quae	quae
gen.	quōrum	quārum	quōrum
dat.	quibus	quibus	quibus
acc.	quōs	quās	quae
abl.	quibus *or*	quibus *or*	quibus *or*
	quīs	quīs	quīs

quīdam (a certain, a) declines like the relative pronoun with the suffix **-dam**:

nom.	quīdam	quaedam	quoddam
acc.	quendam	quandam	quoddam etc.

The interrogative pronoun **quis?** (who?, what?):

nom.	quis?	quis?	quid?
acc.	quem?	quam?	quid? (the rest exactly like the relative pronoun)

The interrogative adjective **quī?** (which?, what?):

nom.	quī?	quae?	quod? (exactly like the relative pronoun)

The indefinite pronoun **aliquis** (someone, something) declines like **quis?** with the prefix **ali-**, except in the nominative singular feminine:

aliquis   aliqua   aliquid etc.

The indefinite pronoun **quisquam, quicquam** (anyone, anything, after a negative) declines like **quis?** with the suffix **-quam**:

nom.	quisquam	quisquam	quicquam

The indefinite pronoun **quisque** (each one individually):

nom.	quisque	quaeque	quidque (quodque) (the rest exactly like **quis**)

Interrogatives, demonstratives, relatives, etc.

quis?, quī? who? which?	**is, ille, iste** (**ista, istud**–like **ille**) that
uter? which of two?	**alter** one or the other of two
quālis? of what kind?	**tālis** of such a kind, such
quālis? how great?	**tantus** so great
quantus? how great?	**hīc** here
ubi? where?	**hinc** from here
	hūc to here, hither
	ibi, illīc, istīc there
unde? from where?	**inde, illinc** from there
quō? to where?	**eō, illō, illūc, istō** to there, thither
quā? by what way?	**eā** by that way

quam? how?*
quandō? when?

quotiēns? how often?
quōmodo? in what way, how?
quārē? why?

tam so*
nunc now
tum, **tunc** then
totiēns so often
ita in that way, thus
idcircō for that reason

* with adjectives and adverbs

| Prepositions

The following take the accusative:

ad	to, towards
ante	before
apud	at, near, among
circum	around
circā, circiter	about
contrā	against
extrā	outside
in	into, on to, to, against
inter	among
intrā	within
iuxtā	next to, beside
per	through
post	after, behind
prope	near
propter	on account of
secundum	along; according to
sub	up to: towards (of time)
super	above
trāns	across
ultrā	beyond

The following take the ablative:

ā/ab	from, by
cōram	in the presence of
cum	with
dē	down from: about
ē/ex	out of
in	in, on
prō	in front of, on behalf of
sine	without
sub	under

| Some expressions with prepositions

Prepositions followed by the accusative:

ad quadrāgintā (or any number)	about 40
nihil ad rem	nothing to do with the matter
ante merīdiem	before midday, a.m.
apud Caesarem (or any person)	at Caesar's house
apud Līuium (or any writer)	in the works of Livy
cōnstat inter omnēs	everyone is agreed
in diēs	from day to day
in uicem	in turn
inter sē pugnant	they fight each other
per deōs	by the gods
per mē licet	I give permission
prope sōlis occāsum	near sunset
sub montem	to the foot of the mountain
sub noctem	just before night

Prepositions followed by the ablative:

ā tergō	from behind
mēcum, tēcum, sēcum, nōbīscum, uōbīscum	with me, with you (sing.), with himself (herself, themselves), with us, with you (pl.)
dē diē in diem	from day to day
dē industriā, ex industriā	on purpose
dē integrō	afresh, anew
prō certō hoc habeō	I am certain about this

| Conjunctions

	Linking sentences or nouns
at, ast	but
atque, ac	and
aut	or
aut ... aut	either ... or
autem*	however, moreover
enim*	for
ergō	and so
et	and
et ... et	both ... and
igitur**	therefore, and so

Linking sentences or nouns

itaque	and so
nam	for
nec/neque	and not, nor
nec/neque ... nec/neque	neither ... nor
-que***	and
sed	but
tamen**	but, however
uel ... uel	either ... or
uērum	however

   * these always come second word in their sentence

  ** these tend to come second word in their sentence

*** translate in front of the Latin word to which it is joined

Subordinating

antequam (ante ... quam)	before
cum	when, since, although
dōnec	until
dum	while, until
etsī	even if, although
nē	lest, that not
nisi, nī	unless
priusquam	before
postquam	after
quamquam	although
quod	because
quoniam	since
sī	if
tametsī	even though
ubi	when
ut + indicative	as, when
ut + subjunctive	1 (in order) that (purpose, command)
	2 (so) that (consequence)

Verbs

1 There are four main patterns into which most Latin verbs fall. We call these patterns **Conjugations** ('joined together' families of verbs). Thus if you learn these four conjugations you will be able to understand and form any part of the vast majority of verbs.

There is a 'mixed conjugation' which takes its endings mainly from the 3rd but partly also from the 4th conjugation.

There are a significant number of irregular verbs and we give the most common of these in the tables of grammar and in the lists of principal parts. The principal parts of active verbs generally consist of four words, 1. the present tense active, 2. the present infinitive active, 3. the perfect tense active, 4. the supine (see below).

In this Grammar, if a verb is given with the numbers 1, 2, 3 or 4 in brackets, this tells you to what conjugation the verb belongs. We give the principal parts of irregular verbs.

2 In the following tables, the numbers 1, 2, and 3 (not in brackets) refer to 'persons'. In the singular 1 is 'I', 2 is 'you', and 3 is 'he', 'she' or 'it'. In the plural, 1 is 'we', 2 is 'you', and 3 is 'they'. (In the principal parts, the present and perfect tenses are given in the first person singular.)

3 Almost all of the terms we use when talking about Latin verbs are used in English grammar. But note the following:

deponent — this is used of verbs which are passive in form but active in meaning, e.g. cōnor (1) (I try) and ūtor (3) (I use). Deponent verbs have no supine and their principal parts consist of 1. the present tense, 2. the present infinitive, 3. the perfect tense.

supine — this is a part of the verb (the fourth of the principal parts) from which other forms of the verb, especially the passive, and also derived nouns can be predicted. It is occasionally used in its own right (see p. 97).

the imperfect tense — this tense usually expresses continuous or repeated or incomplete action in the past, e.g. 'I was doing...' It can also have the meanings 'I began to...' (inceptive) and 'I tried to...' (conative).

the perfect tense — this tense is both a pure perfect tense, e.g. 'I have done ...', and a simple past tense, e.g. 'I did ...' (aorist).

the future perfect tense — 'I shall have done ...', 'you will have done', etc.

a finite verb — a verb in a tense.

indicative — this term tells us that a verb in a tense is not in the subjunctive (see below). It is making a statement.

the subjunctive — the various uses of the subjunctive will become increasingly evident as this Grammar is studied. However, it is worth remarking that the subjunctive is used in English. The following citations are taken from The Oxford English Grammar (published in 1996):
- Israel insists that it *remain* in charge on the borders ...
- If they decide that it's necessary then so *be* it.
- ... you can teach him if *need be*.
- ... more customers are demanding that financial services *be tailored* to their needs.
- He said Sony would not object even if Columbia *were to make* a movie critical of the late Emperor Hirohito.

Words such as 'may', 'might', 'would', 'should', and 'could' can also be helpful when translating the Latin subjunctive.

The subjunctive in a main clause is likely to be:
(a) jussive (giving an order). See p. 89.
(b) a wish:
- **stet haec urbs!** (Cicero, Pro Milone, 33)
- May this city stand!
(c) deliberative (thinking about things):
- **quid agam?**
- What am I to do?
- **quō me nunc uertam?** (Cicero, ad Atticum, 10.12.1)
- Where should I turn to now?

4 The perfect and pluperfect passive indicative and subjunctive, the future perfect passive indicative, the future and perfect participles, and the future infinitive active and perfect infinitive passive are all given in their masculine forms. They are made up of parts of the verb **sum** (I am) and a participle. The participle, being an adjective, must agree with the subject of the verb. Thus, if the subject is feminine or neuter, the ending of the participle will be in the appropriate gender and not the masculine one given in these charts. Compare:

puerī monitī sunt
The boys have been advised

puella monita est
The girl has been advised

uerba dicta sunt
The words have been spoken

1st conjugation—stems in -a

Active Indicative

present	singular	plural
	1 par-ō (*prepare*)	1 parā-mus
	2 parā-s	2 parā-tis
	3 para-t	3 para-nt

future	singular	plural
	1 parā-bō	1 parā-bimus
	2 parā-bis	2 parā-bitis
	3 parā-bit	3 parā-bunt

imperfect	singular	plural
	1 parā-bam	1 parā-bāmus
	2 parā-bās	2 parā-bātis
	3 parā-bat	3 parā-bant

perfect	singular	plural
	1 parāu-ī	1 parāu-imus
	2 parāu-istī	2 parāu-istis
	3 parāu-it	3 parāu-ērunt (-ēre)

future perfect	singular	plural
	1 parāu-erō	1 parāu-erimus
	2 parāu-eris	2 parāu-eritis
	3 parāu-erit	3 parāu-erint

pluperfect	singular	plural
	1 parāu-eram	1 parāu-erāmus
	2 parāu-erās	2 parāu-erātis
	3 parāu-erat	3 parāu-erant

| Active Subjunctive

present	singular	plural
	1 par-em	1 par-ēmus
	2 par-ēs	2 par-ētis
	3 par-et	3 par-ent

imperfect	singular	plural
	1 parār-em	1 parār-ēmus
	2 parār-ēs	2 parār-ētis
	3 parār-et	3 parār-ent

perfect	singular	plural
	1 parāu-erim	1 parāu-erĭmus
	2 parāu-erĭs	2 parāu-erĭtis
	3 parāu-erit	3 parāu-erint

pluperfect	singular	plural
	1 parāu-issem	1 parāu-issēmus
	2 parāu-issēs	2 parāu-issētis
	3 parāu-isset	3 parāu-issent

| Other forms

Imperative	singular	plural	
	parā	parāte	

Infinitives	present	perfect	future
	parāre	parāuisse (parāsse)	parātūrus esse

Participles	present	future	
	parāns	parātūrus	

| Gerund | parandum | **Supine** | parātum |

2nd conjugation—stems in -e

Active Indicative

present	singular	plural
	1 mone-ō (*advise, warn*)	1 monē-mus
	2 monē-s	2 monē-tis
	3 mone-t	3 mone-nt

future	singular	plural
	1 monē-bō	1 monē-bimus
	2 monē-bis	2 monē-bitis
	3 monē-bit	3 monē-bunt

imperfect	singular	plural
	1 monē-bam	1 monē-bāmus
	2 monē-bās	2 monē-bātis
	3 monē-bat	3 monē-bant

perfect	singular	plural
	1 monu-ī	1 monu-imus
	2 monu-istī	2 monu-istis
	3 monu-it	3 monu-ērunt (-ēre)

future perfect	singular	plural
	1 monu-erō	1 monu-erimus
	2 monu-eris	2 monu-eritis
	3 monu-erit	3 monu-erint

pluperfect	singular	plural
	1 monu-eram	1 monu-erāmus
	2 monu-erās	2 monu-erātis
	3 monu-erat	3 monu-erant

| Active Subjunctive

present	singular	plural
	1 mone-am	1 mone-āmus
	2 mone-ās	2 mone-ātis
	3 mone-at	3 mone-ant

imperfect	singular	plural
	1 monēr-em	1 monēr-ēmus
	2 monēr-ēs	2 monēr-ētis
	3 monēr-et	3 monēr-ent

perfect	singular	plural
	1 monu-erim	1 monu-erĭmus
	2 monu-erĭs	2 monu-erĭtis
	3 monu-erit	3 monu-erint

pluperfect	singular	plural
	1 monu-issem	1 monu-issēmus
	2 monu-issēs	2 monu-issētis
	3 monu-isset	3 monu-issent

| Other forms

Imperative	singular	plural
	monē	monēte

Infinitives	present	perfect	future
	monēre	monuisse	monitūrus esse

Participles	present	future
	monēns	monitūrus

Gerund	monendum	**Supine**	monitum

3rd conjugation—stems in consonants

Active Indicative

present	singular	plural
	1 reg-ō (*rule*)	1 reg-imus
	2 reg-is	2 reg-itis
	3 reg-it	3 reg-unt

future	singular	plural
	1 reg-am	1 reg-ēmus
	2 reg-ēs	2 reg-ētis
	3 reg-et	3 reg-ent

imperfect	singular	plural
	1 regē-bam	1 regē-bāmus
	2 regē-bās	2 regē-bātis
	3 regē-bat	3 regē-bant

perfect	singular	plural
	1 rēx-ī	1 rēx-imus
	2 rēx-istī	2 rēx-istis
	3 rēx-it	3 rēx-ērunt (-ēre)

future perfect	singular	plural
	1 rēx-erō	1 rēx-erimus
	2 rēx-eris	2 rēx-eritis
	3 rēx-erit	3 rēx-erint

pluperfect	singular	plural
	1 rēx-eram	1 rēx-erāmus
	2 rēx-erās	2 rēx-erātis
	3 rēx-erat	3 rēx-erant

| Active Subjunctive

present	singular	plural
	1 reg-am	1 reg-āmus
	2 reg-ās	2 reg-ātis
	3 reg-at	3 reg-ant

imperfect	singular	plural
	1 reger-em	1 reger-ēmus
	2 reger-ēs	2 reger-ētis
	3 reger-et	3 reger-ent

perfect	singular	plural
	1 rēx-erim	1 rēx-erĭmus
	2 rēx-erĭs	2 rēx-erĭtis
	3 rēx-erit	3 rēx-erint

pluperfect	singular	plural
	1 rēx-issem	1 rēx-issēmus
	2 rēx-issēs	2 rēx-issētis
	3 rēx-isset	3 rēx-issent

| Other forms

Imperative	singular	plural
	1 rege	regite

Infinitives	present	perfect	future
	regere	rēxisse	rēctūrus esse

Participles	present	future
	regēns	rēctūrus

Gerund	regendum	**Supine**	rēctum

4th conjugation—stems in -i

Active Indicative

present	singular	plural
	1 audi-ō (*hear*)	1 audī-mus
	2 audī-s	2 audī-tis
	3 audi-t	3 audi-unt

future	singular	plural
	1 audi-am	1 audi-ēmus
	2 audi-ēs	2 audi-ētis
	3 audi-et	3 audi-ent

imperfect	singular	plural
	1 audiē-bam	1 audiē-bāmus
	2 audiē-bās	2 audiē-bātis
	3 audiē-bat	3 audiē-bant

perfect	singular	plural
	1 audīu-ī	1 audīu-imus
	2 audīu-istī	2 audīu-istis
	3 audīu-it	3 audīu-ērunt (-ēre)

future perfect	singular	plural
	1 audīu-erō	1 audīu-erimus
	2 audīu-eris	2 audīu-eritis
	3 audīu-erit	3 audīu-erint

pluperfect	singular	plural
	1 audīu-eram	1 audīu-erāmus
	2 audīu-erās	2 audīu-erātis
	3 audīu-erat	3 audīu-erant

| Active Subjunctive

present	singular	plural
	1 audi-am	1 audi-āmus
	2 audi-ās	2 audi-ātis
	3 audi-at	3 audi-ant

imperfect	singular	plural
	1 audīr-em	1 audīr-ēmus
	2 audīr-ēs	2 audīr-ētis
	3 audīr-et	3 audīr-ent

perfect	singular	plural
	1 audīu-erim	1 audīu-erĭmus
	2 audīu-erĭs	2 audīu-erĭtis
	3 audīu-erit	3 audīu-erint

pluperfect	singular	plural
	1 audīu-issem	1 audīu-issēmus
	2 audīu-issēs	2 audīu-issētis
	3 audīu-isset	3 audīu-issent

| Other forms

Imperative	singular	plural	
	audī	audīte	

Infinitives	present	perfect	future
	audīre	audīuisse (audīsse)	audītūrus esse

Participles	present	future	
	audiēns	audītūrus	

Gerund	audiendum	Supine	audītum

| Mixed conjugation

| Active Indicative

present	singular	plural
	1 capi-ō (*take*)	1 capi-mus
	2 capi-s	2 capi-tis
	3 capi-t	3 capi-unt

future	singular	plural
	1 capi-am	1 capi-ēmus
	2 capi-ēs	2 capi-ētis
	3 capi-et	3 capi-ent

imperfect	singular	plural
	1 capiē-bam	1 capiē-bāmus
	2 capiē-bās	2 capiē-bātis
	3 capiē-bat	3 capiē-bant

perfect	singular	plural
	1 cēp-ī	1 cēp-imus
	2 cēp-istī	2 cēp-istis
	3 cēp-it	3 cēp-ērunt (ēre)

future perfect	singular	plural
	1 cēp-erō	1 cēp-erimus
	2 cēp-eris	2 cēp-eritis
	3 cēp-erit	3 cēp-erint

pluperfect	singular	plural
	1 cēp-eram	1 cēp-erāmus
	2 cēp-erās	2 cēp-erātis
	3 cēp-erat	3 cēp-erant

| Active Subjunctive

present	singular	plural
	1 capi-am	1 capi-āmus
	2 capi-ās	2 capi-ātis
	3 capi-at	3 capi-ant

imperfect	singular	plural
	1 caper-em	1 caper-ēmus
	2 caper-ēs	2 caper-ētis
	3 caper-et	3 caper-ent

perfect	singular	plural
	1 cēp-erim	1 cēp-erĭmus
	2 cēp-erĭs	2 cēp-erĭtis
	3 cēp-erit	3 cēp-erint

pluperfect	singular	plural
	1 cēp-issem	1 cēp-issēmus
	2 cēp-issēs	2 cēp-issētis
	3 cēp-isset	3 cēp-issent

| Other forms

Imperative	singular	plural
	cape	capite

Infinitives	present	perfect	future
	capere	cēpisse	captūrus esse

Participles	present	future
	capiēns	captūrus

Gerund	capiendum	Supine	captum

1st conjugation—stems in -a

Passive Indicative

present	singular	plural
	1 par-or	1 parā-mur
	2 parā-ris	2 parā-minī
	3 parā-tur	3 para-ntur

future	singular	plural
	1 parā-bor	1 parā-bimur
	2 parā-beris	2 parā-biminī
	3 parā-bitur	3 parā-buntur

imperfect	singular	plural
	1 parā-bar	1 parā-bāmur
	2 parā-bāris	2 parā-bāminī
	3 parā-bātur	3 parā-bantur

perfect	singular	plural
	1 parātus sum	1 parātī sumus
	2 parātus es	2 parātī estis
	3 parātus est	3 parātī sunt

future perfect	singular	plural
	1 parātus erō	1 parātī erimus
	2 parātus eris	2 parātī eritis
	3 parātus erit	3 parātī erunt

pluperfect	singular	plural
	1 parātus eram	1 parātī erāmus
	2 parātus erās	2 parātī erātis
	3 parātus erat	3 parātī erant

| Passive Subjunctive

present	singular	plural
	1 par-er	1 par-ēmur
	2 par-ēris	2 par-ēminī
	3 par-ētur	3 par-entur

imperfect	singular	plural
	1 parār-er	1 parār-ēmur
	2 parār-ēris	2 parār-ēminī
	3 parār-ētur	3 parār-entur

perfect	singular	plural
	1 parātus sim	1 parātī sīmus
	2 parātus sīs	2 parātī sītis
	3 parātus sit	3 parātī sint

pluperfect	singular	plural
	1 parātus essem	1 parātī essēmus
	2 parātus essēs	2 parātī essētis
	3 parātus esset	3 parātī essent

| Other forms

Imperative	singular	plural
	parāre	[parāminī]

Infinitives	present	perfect	future
	parārī	parātus esse	parātum īrī

Participle	perfect	Gerundive	parandus
	parātus		

2nd conjugation—stems in -e

Passive Indicative

present	singular	plural
	1 mone-or	1 monē-mur
	2 monē-ris	2 monē-minī
	3 monē-tur	3 mone-ntur

future	singular	plural
	1 monē-bor	1 monē-bimur
	2 monē-beris	2 monē-biminī
	3 monē-bitur	3 monē-buntur

imperfect	singular	plural
	1 monē-bar	1 monē-bāmur
	2 monē-bāris	2 monē-bāminī
	3 monē-bātur	3 monē-bantur

perfect	singular	plural
	1 monitus sum	1 monitī sumus
	2 monitus es	2 monitī estis
	3 monitus est	3 monitī sunt

future perfect	singular	plural
	1 monitus erō	1 monitī erimus
	2 monitus eris	2 monitī eritis
	3 monitus erit	3 monitī erunt

pluperfect	singular	plural
	1 monitus eram	1 monitī erāmus
	2 monitus erās	2 monitī erātis
	3 monitus erat	3 monitī erant

| Passive Subjunctive

present	singular	plural
	1 mone-ar	1 mone-āmur
	2 mone-āris	2 mone-āminī
	3 mone-ātur	3 mone-antur

imperfect	singular	plural
	1 monēr-er	1 monēr-ēmur
	2 monēr-ēris	2 monēr-ēminī
	3 monēr-ētur	3 monēr-entur

perfect	singular	plural
	1 monitus sim	1 monitī sīmus
	2 monitus sīs	2 monitī sītis
	3 monitus sit	3 monitī sint

pluperfect	singular	plural
	1 monitus essem	1 monitī essēmus
	2 monitus essēs	2 monitī essētis
	3 monitus esset	3 monitī essent

| Other forms

Imperative	singular	plural
	monēre	[monēminī]

Infinitives	present	perfect	future
	monērī	monitus esse	monitum īrī

Participles	perfect	**Gerundive**	monendus
	monitus		

3rd conjugation—stems in consonants

Passive Indicative

present	singular	plural
	1 reg-or	1 reg-imur
	2 reg-eris	2 reg-iminī
	3 reg-itur	3 reg-untur

future	singular	plural
	1 reg-ar	1 reg-ēmur
	2 reg-ēris	2 reg-ēminī
	3 reg-ētur	3 reg-entur

imperfect	singular	plural
	1 reg-ēbar	1 reg-ēbāmur
	2 reg-ēbāris	2 reg-ēbāminī
	3 reg-ēbātur	3 reg-ēbantur

perfect	singular	plural
	1 rēctus sum	1 rēctī sumus
	2 rēctus es	2 rēctī estis
	3 rēctus est	3 rēctī sunt

future perfect	singular	plural
	1 rēctus erō	1 rēctī erimus
	2 rēctus eris	2 rēctī eritis
	3 rēctus erit	3 rēctī erunt

pluperfect	singular	plural
	1 rēctus eram	1 rēctī erāmus
	2 rēctus erās	2 rēctī erātis
	3 rēctus erat	3 rēctī erant

| Passive Subjunctive

present	singular	plural
	1 reg-ar	1 reg-āmur
	2 reg-āris	2 reg-āminī
	3 reg-ātur	3 reg-antur

imperfect	singular	plural
	1 reger-er	1 reger-ēmur
	2 reger-ēris	2 reger-ēminī
	3 reger-ētur	3 reger-entur

perfect	singular	plural
	1 rēctus sim	1 rēctī sīmus
	2 rēctus sīs	2 rēctī sītis
	3 rēctus sit	3 rēctī sint

pluperfect	singular	plural
	1 rēctus essem	1 rēctī essēmus
	2 rēctus essēs	2 rēctī essētis
	3 rēctus esset	3 rēctī essent

| Other forms

Imperative	singular	plural
	regere	[regiminī]

Infinitives	present	perfect	future
	regī	rēctus esse	rēctum īrī

Participles	perfect	**Gerundive**	regendus
	rēctus		

4th conjugation—stems in -i

Passive Indicative

present	singular	plural
	1 audi-or	1 audī-mur
	2 audī-ris	2 audī-minī
	3 audī-tur	3 audi-untur

future	singular	plural
	1 audi-ar	1 audi-ēmur
	2 audi-ēris	2 audi-ēminī
	3 audi-ētur	3 audi-entur

imperfect	singular	plural
	1 audi-ēbar	1 audi-ēbāmur
	2 audi-ēbāris	2 audi-ēbāminī
	3 audi-ēbātur	3 audi-ēbantur

perfect	singular	plural
	1 audītus sum	1 audītī sumus
	2 audītus es	2 audītī estis
	3 audītus est	3 audītī sunt

future perfect	singular	plural
	1 audītus erō	1 audītī erimus
	2 audītus eris	2 audītī eritis
	3 audītus erit	3 audītī erunt

pluperfect	singular	plural
	1 audītus eram	1 audītī erāmus
	2 audītus erās	2 audītī erātis
	3 audītus erat	3 audītī erant

| Passive Subjunctive

present	singular	plural
	1 audi-ar	1 audi-āmur
	2 audi-āris	2 audi-āminī
	3 audi-ātur	3 audi-antur

imperfect	singular	plural
	1 audīr-er	1 audīr-ēmur
	2 audīr-ēris	2 audīr-ēminī
	3 audīr-ētur	3 audīr-entur

perfect	singular	plural
	1 audītus sim	1 audītī sīmus
	2 audītus sīs	2 audītī sītis
	3 audītus sit	3 audītī sint

pluperfect	singular	plural
	1 audītus essem	1 audītī essēmus
	2 audītus essēs	2 audītī essētis
	3 audītus esset	3 audītī essent

| Other forms

Imperative	singular	plural
	audīre	[audīminī]

Infinitives	present	perfect	future
	audīrī	audītus esse	audītum īrī

Participles	perfect	**Gerundive**	audiendus
	audītus		

| Mixed conjugation

| Passive Indicative

present	singular	plural
	1 capi-or	1 cap-imur
	2 cap-eris	2 cap-iminī
	3 cap-itur	3 capi-untur

future	singular	plural
	1 capi-ar	1 capi-ēmur
	2 capi-ēris	2 capi-ēminī
	3 capi-ētur	3 capi-entur

imperfect	singular	plural
	1 capi-ēbar	1 capi-ēbāmur
	2 capi-ēbāris	2 capi-ēbāminī
	3 capi-ēbātur	3 capi-ēbantur

perfect	singular	plural
	1 captus sum	1 captī sumus
	2 captus es	2 captī estis
	3 captus est	3 captī sunt

future perfect	singular	plural
	1 captus erō	1 captī erimus
	2 captus eris	2 captī eritis
	3 captus erit	3 captī erunt

pluperfect	singular	plural
	1 captus eram	1 captī erāmus
	2 captus erās	2 captī erātis
	3 captus erat	3 captī erant

| Passive Subjunctive

present	singular	plural
	1 capi-ar	1 capi-āmur
	2 capi-āris	2 capi-āminī
	3 capi-ātur	3 capi-antur

imperfect	singular	plural
	1 caper-er	1 caper-ēmur
	2 caper-ēris	2 caper-ēminī
	3 caper-ētur	3 caper-entur

perfect	singular	plural
	1 captus sim	1 captī sīmus
	2 captus sīs	2 captī sītis
	3 captus sit	3 captī sint

pluperfect	singular	plural
	1 captus essem	1 captī essēmus
	2 captus essēs	2 captī essētis
	3 captus esset	3 captī essent

| Other forms

Imperative	singular	plural
	capere	[capiminī]

Infinitives	present	perfect	future
	capī	captus esse	captum īrī

Participles	perfect
	captus

Gerundive	capiendus

| Deponent verbs (passive in form, active in meaning)

	Indicative	Subjunctive
present	cōnor (*try*)	cōner
future	cōnābor	
imperfect	cōnābar	cōnārer
perfect	cōnātus sum	cōnātus sim
future perfect	cōnātus erō	
pluperfect	cōnātus eram	cōnātus essem

	Imperative
singular	cōnāre
plural	[cōnāminī]

	Infinitives
present	cōnārī
perfect	cōnātus esse
future	cōnātūrus esse

	Participles
present	cōnāns
perfect	cōnātus
future	cōnātūrus

Gerund
cōnandum

Gerundive
cōnandus

Irregular verbs

Indicatives		sum: I am	possum: I am able	eō: I go
present				
singular				
	1	sum	possum	eō
	2	es	potes	īs
	3	est	potest	it
plural				
	1	sumus	possumus	īmus
	2	estis	potestis	ītis
	3	sunt	possunt	eunt
future				
singular				
	1	erō	pot-erō	ī-bō
	2	eris	pot-eris	ī-bis
	3	erit	pot-erit	ī-bit
plural				
	1	erimus	pot-erimus	ī-bimus
	2	eritis	pot-eritis	ī-bitis
	3	erunt	pot-erunt	ī-bunt
imperfect				
singular				
	1	eram	pot-eram	ī-bam
	2	erās	pot-erās	ī-bās
	3	erat	pot-erat	ī-bat
plural				
	1	erāmus	pot-erāmus	ī-bāmus
	2	erātis	pot-erātis	ī-bātis
	3	erant	pot-erant	ī-bant

perfect	*stem* **fu-**	**potu-**	**i-**	**īu-**
singular				
1	fu-ī	potu-ī	i-ī or	īu-ī
2	fu-istī	potu-istī	īstī	īu-istī
3	fu-it	potu-it	i-it	īu-it

perfect	*stem* fu-	potu-	i-	īu-
plural				
1	fu-imus	potu-imus	i-imus	īu-imus
2	fu-istis	potu-istis	īstis	īu-istis
3	fu-ērunt	potu-ērunt	i-ērunt	īu-ērunt
	(-ēre)	(-ēre)	(-ēre)	

future perfect

	fu-erō etc.	potu-erō etc.	i-erō etc.	

pluperfect

	fu-eram etc.	potu-eram etc.	i-eram etc.	

Subjunctives

present

	sim etc.	possim etc.	eam etc.	

imperfect

	essem etc.	possem etc.	īrem etc.	

perfect

	fu-erim etc.	potu-erim etc.	i-erim etc., īu-erim etc.	

pluperfect

	fu-issem etc.	potu-issem etc.	īssem etc., īu-issem etc.	

Imperative

singular

	es, estō	—	ī	

plural

	este	—	īte	

Infinitives

present

	esse	posse	īre	

perfect

	fuisse	potuisse	īsse	

future

futūrus esse, fore	—	itūrus esse

Participle

present

—	[potēns]	iēns, euntis

future

futūrus	—	itūrus

Gerund

—	—	eundum

uolō, uelle, uoluī	I wish, I am willing
nōlō, nōlle, nōluī	I am unwilling, I refuse
mālō, mālle, māluī	I prefer
ferō, ferre, tulī, lātum	I carry, bear

present **active** **passive**

singular

1 uolō	nōlō	mālō	ferō	feror
2 uīs	nōn uīs	māuīs	fers	ferris
3 uult	nōn uult	māuult	fert	fertur

plural

1 uolumus	nōlumus	mālumus	ferimus	ferimur
2 uultis	nōn uultis	māuultis	fertis	feriminī
3 uolunt	nōlunt	mālunt	ferunt	feruntur

future

singular

1 uolam	nōlam	mālam	feram	ferar
2 uolēs	nōlēs	mālēs	ferēs	ferēris
3 uolet etc.	nōlet etc.	mālet etc.	feret etc.	ferētur etc

imperfect

uolēbam etc.	nōlēbam etc.	mālēbam etc.	ferēbam. etc.	ferēbar etc.

perfect

uoluī etc.	nōluī etc.	māluī etc.	tulī etc.	lātus sum etc.

				active	passive
future perfect					
	uoluerō etc.	nōluerō etc.	māluerō etc.	tulerō etc.	lātus erō etc.
pluperfect					
	uolueram etc.	nōlueram etc.	mālueram etc.	tuleram etc.	lātus eram etc.

subjunctives

present					
	uelim etc.	nōlim etc.	mālim etc.	feram etc.	ferar etc.
imperfect					
	uellem etc.	nōllem etc.	māllem etc.	ferrem etc.	ferrer etc.
perfect					
	uoluerim etc.	nōluerim etc.	māluerim etc.	tulerim etc.	lātus erim etc.
pluperfect					
	uoluissem etc.	nōluissem etc.	māluissem etc.	tulissem etc.	lātus essem etc.

Imperative

	—	nōlī	—	fer	[ferre]
	—	nōlīte	—	ferte	—

Infinitives

present					
	uelle	nōlle	mālle	ferre	ferrī
perfect					
	uoluisse	nōluisse	māluisse	tulisse	lātus esse
future					
	—	—	—	lātūrus esse	lātum īrī

Participles

present

uolēns	nōlēns	—	ferēns	—

perfect

—	—	—	—	lātus

future

—	—	—	lātūrus	—

Gerund

—	—	—	ferendum	—

Gerundive

—	—	—	—	ferendus

fīō, fierī   I become, I am made

This verb only exists in the present, future, and imperfect and takes the place of the equivalent passive forms of **faciō** (I make).

	indicative	subjunctive
singular		
1	fīō	fīam
2	fīs	fīās
3	fit	fīat
plural		
1	[fīmus]	fīāmus
2	[fītis]	fīātis
3	fīunt	fīant
future		
1	fīam	
2	fīēs	
3	fīet etc.	

imperfect

1	fīēbam	fierem
2	fīēbās	fierēs
3	fīēbat etc.	fieret etc.

Principal parts of verbs: 1st, 2nd and 4th conjugations

Regular verbs

	present	infinitive	perfect	supine
1st	parō	parāre	parāuī	parātum
2nd	moneō	monēre	monuī	monitum
4th	audiō	audīre	audīuī	audītum

The following are irregular:

1st conjugation

1 Perfect -uī

    cubō, cubāre, cubuī, cubitum   I lie down
    domō, domāre, domuī, domitum   I tame
    secō, secāre, secuī, sectum   I cut
    uetō, uetāre, uetuī, uetitum   I forbid

2 Perfect with lengthened vowel

    iuuō, iuuāre, iūuī iūtum   I help
    lauō, lauāre, lāuī, lautum, or lōtum   I wash

3 Reduplicated perfect

    dō, dare, dedī, datum   I give
    stō, stāre, stetī, statum   I stand

2nd conjugation

1 Perfect -uī, supine -tum or -sum

    cēnseō, cēnsēre, cēnsuī, cēnsum   I judge, vote
    doceō, docēre, docuī, doctum   I teach
    teneō, tenēre, tenuī, tentum   I hold

2 Perfect **-ēuī**

dēleō, dēlēre, dēlēuī, dēlētum	I destroy
fleō, flēre, flēuī, flētum	I weep

3 Perfect **-sī**

ardeō, ardēre, arsī	I burn, am on fire
augeō, augēre, auxī, auctum	I increase
fulgeō, fulgēre, fulsī	I shine
iubeō, iubēre, iussī, iussum	I order
lūceō, lūcēre, lūxī	I shine
lūgeō, lūgēre, lūxī	I mourn
maneō, manēre, mānsī, mānsum	I stay, remain
rīdeō, rīdēre, rīsī, rīsum	I laugh
suādeō, suādēre, suāsī, suāsum + dat.	I persuade
torqueō, torquēre, torsī, tortum	I twist, torture

4 Perfect with lengthened vowel

caueō, cauēre, cāuī, cautum	I beware
faueō, fauēre, fāuī, fautum + dat.	I favour
foueō, fouēre, fōuī, fōtum	I cherish, look after
moueō, mouēre, mōuī, mōtum	I move
sedeō, sedēre, sēdī, sessum	I sit
uideō, uidēre, uīdī, uīsum	I see
uoueō, uouēre, uōuī, uōtum	I vow

5 Verbs with reduplicated perfect

mordeō, mordēre, momordī, morsum	I bite
pendeō, pendēre, pependī	I hang
spondeō, spondēre, spopondī, spōnsum	I pledge
but **respondeō, respondēre, respondī, respōnsum**	I answer

····▶ **Note**

Compound verbs do not have reduplicated perfects, except for compounds of **dō** (I give) and **stō** (I stand).

4th conjugation

1 Perfect in **-uī**

aperiō, aperīre, aperuī, apertum	I open
operiō, operīre, operuī, opertum	I cover
saliō, salīre, saluī	I dance

2 Perfect in **-sī**

sentiō, sentīre, sēnsī, sēnsum	I feel
uinciō, uincīre, uīnxī, uīnctum	I bind

3 Perfect with lengthened vowel

ueniō, uenīre, uēnī, uentum	I come

3rd conjugation

1a Perfect **-sī**, supine **-tum**

carpō, carpere, carpsī, carptum	I pick
cingō, cingere, cīnxī, cīnctum	I surround
dīcō, dīcere, dīxī, dictum	I say, tell
dūcō, dūcere, dūxī, ductum	I lead
fingō, fingere, fīnxī, fictum	I shape, pretend
gerō, gerere, gessī, gestum	I carry, wear
intellegō, intellegere, intellēxī, intellēctum	I understand
iungō, iungere, iūnxī, iūnctum	I join
neglegō, neglegere, neglēxī, neglēctum	I neglect
nūbō, nūbere, nūpsī, nūptum	I marry
regō, regere, rēxī, rēctum	I rule
scrībō, scrībere, scrīpsī, scrīptum	I write
sūmō, sūmere, sūmpsī, sūmptum	I take
surgō, surgere, surrēxī, surrēctum	I rise, get up (a compound of **regō**)
tegō, tegere, tēxī, tēctum	I cover
trahō, trahere, trāxī, tractum	I drag
uehō, uehere, uēxī, uectum	I carry
uīuō, uīuere, uīxī, uīctum	I live

····▶ **Note**

regō, **surgō**, **tegō**, **trahō**, **uehō** and their compounds lengthen the vowel of the stem in the perfect.

1b Perfect **-sī**, supine **-sum**

cēdō, cēdere, cessī, cessum	I withdraw, yield ('go' in compounds)
claudō, claudere, clausī, clausum	I shut
ēuādō, ēuādere, ēuāsī, ēuāsum	I escape
laedō, laedere, laesī, laesum	I hurt, harm
lūdō, lūdere, lūsī, lūsum	I play
mittō, mittere, mīsī, missum	I send
plaudō, plaudere, plausī, plausum	I clap, applaud

····▶ Note

1. This is especially common with verbs whose roots end in **-t** or **-d**.
2. Compound verbs usually form the perfect in the same way as the simple verb, e.g. **prōcēdō, prōcēdere, prōcessī, prōcessum** (I go forward), **remittō, remittere, remīsī, remissum** (I send back). But some compounds opt for a perfect in **-sī** even when the simple verb has another formation, e.g. **intellegō** (simple verb **legō**, see **3** below).

2a Perfect stem the same as the present, supine **-tum**

cōnstituō, cōnstituere, cōnstituī, cōnstitūtum	I decide
induō, induere, induī, indūtum	I put on
metuō, metuere, metuī, metūtum	I fear
soluō, soluere, soluī, solūtum	I loose
uoluō, uoluere, uoluī, uolūtum	I roll

2b Perfect stem the same as the present, supine **-sum**

accendō, accendere, accendī, accēnsum	I light (a fire)
ascendō, ascendere, ascendī, ascēnsum	I climb
dēscendō, dēscendere, dēscendī, dēscēnsum	I climb down
dēfendō, dēfendere, dēfendī, dēfēnsum	I defend
uertō, uertere, uertī, uersum	I turn

2c Perfect stem the same as the present but no supine

bibō, bibere, bibī	I drink
uīsō, uīsere, uīsī	I go to see

3 Verbs showing a lengthened vowel in the perfect, supine **-tum**

agō, agere, ēgī, āctum	I do, I drive
cōgō, cōgere, coēgī, coāctum	I drive together, I compel
emō, emere, ēmī, ēmptum	I buy
legō, legere, lēgī, lēctum	I read, I gather
frangō*, frangere, frēgī, frāctum	I break
relinquō*, relinquere, relīquī, relictum	I leave
rumpō*, rumpere, rūpī, ruptum	I burst open
uincō*, uincere, uīcī, uictum	I conquer

····▶ Note

Verbs marked* insert **n** (**m** before **p**) in the present, which is dropped in perfect and supine, e.g. **fra-n-gō**, original stem **frag-**, hence **frēgī, frāctum**.

4a Verbs with reduplicated perfect, supine **-tum**

Compound verbs do not have reduplicated perfects, except for compounds of **dō** (I give) and **stō** (I stand).

addō, addere, addidī, additum	I add (so all compounds of **dō**)
canō, canere, cecinī, cantum	I sing
(cōn)sistō, (cōn)sistere, (cōn)stitī, (cōn)stitum	I stand
tangō, tangere, tetigī, tāctum	I touch
tendō, tendere, tetendī, tentum or **tēnsum**	I stretch
but **contendō, contendere, contendī, contentum**	I march, hasten

4b Verbs with reduplicated perfect, supine **-sum**

cadō, cadere, cecidī, cāsum	I fall
caedō, caedere, cecīdī, caesum	I beat, kill
currō, currere, cucurrī, cursum	I run
discō, discere, didicī	I learn
parcō, parcere, pepercī, parsum + dat.	I spare
pellō, pellere, pepulī, pulsum	I drive
poscō, poscere, poposcī	I demand

····▶ **Note**

Compounds of **cadō, caedō, currō** and **pellō** do not have reduplicated perfects, e.g.

occidō, occidere, occidī, occāsum	I fall down, die
occīdō, occīdere, occīdī, occīsum	I kill
occurrō, occurrere, occurrī, occursum	I run to meet, meet
expellō, expellere, expulī, expulsum	I drive out

5a Verbs forming perfect **-uī**

arcessō, arcessere, arcessīuī, arcessītum	I summon
colō, colere, coluī, cultum	l cultivate
petō, petere, petīuī, petītum	I seek
pōnō, pōnere, posuī, positum	I place
quaerō, quaerere, quaesīuī, quaesītum	I ask, seek
sinō, sinere, sīuī, situm	I allow
but **dēsinō, dēsinere, dēsiī, dēsitum**	I cease
spernō, spernere, sprēuī, sprētum	I despise

5b Inceptive verbs (i.e. verbs which express the beginnings of actions)

····▶ **Note**

The present of these verbs is formed with a suffix **-scō** that is not an essential part of the verbal stem.

cognōscō, cognōscere, cognōuī, cognitum	I get to know, learn
crēscō, crēscere, crēuī, crētum	I grow
nōscō, nōscere, nōuī, nōtum	I get to know
quiēscō, quiēscere, quiēuī, quiētum	I rest

| Mixed conjugation

capiō, capere, cēpī, captum	I take
cupiō, cupere, cupīuī, cupītum	I desire
faciō, facere, fēcī, factum	I make, do
fugiō, fugere, fūgī	I flee
iaciō iacere, iēcī, iactum	I throw
rapiō, rapere, rapuī, raptum	I seize
(īn)spiciō, (īn)spicere, (īn)spexī, (īn)spectum	I look at

| Deponent verbs

1st conjugation (all regular)

cōnor, cōnārī, cōnātus sum	I try

2nd conjugation

cōnfīteor, cōnfītērī, cōnfessus sum	I confess
reor, rērī, ratus sum	I think
uereor, uerērī, ueritus sum	I fear

3rd conjugation

amplector, amplectī, amplexus sum	I embrace
fruor, fruī, frūctus sum + abl.	I enjoy
fungor, fungī, fūnctus sum + abl.	I perform
lābor, lābī, lāpsus sum	I slip, glide
loquor, loquī, locūtus sum	I speak
queror, querī, questus sum	I complain
sequor, sequī, secūtus sum	I follow

····▶ **Note**

The present of these verbs is formed with a suffix in **-scor** that is not an essential part of the verb stem.

īrāscor, īrāscī, īrātus sum + dat.	I am angry (with)
nancīscor, nancīscī, nactus (or nānctus) sum	I obtain
nāscor, nāscī, nātus sum	I am born
nītor, nītī, nīxus sum (or nīsus) sum	I lean on, strive
oblīuīscor, oblīuīscī, oblītus sum + gen.	I forget
proficīscor, proficīscī, profectus sum	I set out
reuertor, reuertī, reuersus sum	I return
ūtor, ūtī, ūsus sum + abl.	I use

4th conjugation

experior, experīrī, expertus sum	I try
ordior, ordīrī, orsus sum	I begin
orior, orīrī, ortus sum	I arise
potior, potīrī, potītus sum often + abl.	I acquire, possess

Mixed conjugation

gradior, gradī, gressus sum	I walk
morior, morī, mortuus sum (fut. part. **moritūrus**)	I die
patior, patī, passus sum	I suffer
prōgredior, prōgredī, prōgressus sum	I advance

| Semi-deponent verbs

2nd conjugation

audeō, audēre, ausus sum	I dare
gaudeō, gaudēre, gāuīsus sum	I rejoice
soleō, solēre, solitus sum	I am accustomed

3rd conjugation

cōnfīdō, cōnfīdere, cōnfīsus sum + dat.	I trust

Irregular

fīō, fierī, factus sum	I am made, I become

Relative clauses

She is the woman <u>who</u> betrayed me.
I am the man <u>whom</u> she betrayed.
There is the man <u>for whom</u> she left me.
This is the house <u>that</u> Jack built.

The relative pronoun (who, which, whom, that) is one of the English words which can change according to its function in the sentence. Note, however, that in English the word 'whom' is now used very little. The third of the three sentences above could be rephrased:

There is the man (<u>who/that</u>) she left me for.

As you can see, the word 'who', 'whom' or 'that' may be omitted in English. (The relative pronoun cannot be omitted in Latin.)

The relative pronoun refers back to a noun or pronoun, in the above sentences 'woman', 'man', 'man', and 'house' respectively. We call this word the *antecedent*.

In Latin the word for 'who' is **quī, quae, quod** (see pp. 27–8). It agrees in gender and number with its antecedent, but its case depends on its function in the clause which it introduces.

epistulam accēpī quam tū mihi mīserās.
I received the letter <u>which</u> you had sent me.

ille quī tibi epistulam mīsit nōn tē prōdet.
The man <u>who</u> sent you the letter will not betray you.

ille est amīcus cui epistulam mīsī.
He is the friend <u>to whom</u> I sent the letter.

In the first sentence **quam** is feminine and singular because it agrees with its antecedent **epistulam** in gender and number. It is accusative, *not* because **epistulam** is accusative, but because it is the object of the verb 'had sent'.

In the second sentence, **quī** is masculine and singular because it agrees with its antecedent **ille** in gender and number. It is nominative *not* because **ille** is nominative, but because it is the subject of the verb 'sent'.

If you are translating from English into Latin, you can always discover the case of the relative pronoun by phrasing the English relative clause as a full sentence. In the first sentence above, you can change 'which you had sent me' to 'You had sent me it (the letter)'. It would be accusative in Latin. The Latin word for 'letter' is feminine and singular. Hence *quam*. In the third sentence, 'to whom I sent the letter' can be rephrased 'I sent the letter to him': dative, masculine, and singular. Hence *cui*.

Practice sentences

Translate into English or Latin as appropriate:

1. **uxor quae bona est ūnō uirō est contenta.**
2. **hoc illīs nārrō quī mē nōn intellegunt.** (Phaedrus, 3.128)
3. **iste est amīcus ā quō prōditus sum.**
4. **mātrēs quārum līberōs Rōmānī trucīdāuērunt miserrimae erant.**
5. Give me a man who loves women.
6. He is a friend without whom I am unwilling to leave the city.
7. The children I gave the money to were very happy.
8. He is a man whom I try to avoid.

Time, place, and space

| Time

- In Latin the *accusative* expresses 'time how long':

  tōtam noctem dormīuī.
  I slept the whole night.

  septem hōrās uiātōrēs ambulābant.
  The travellers were walking for seven hours.

Note: **puella quīnque annōs nāta**
  a girl five years old (*literally*, a girl born for five years)

- The *ablative* expresses 'time when':

  domum tuam secundā hōrā ueniam.
  I shall come to your house at the second hour.

  paucīs post diēbus Capuam aduēnērunt.
  A few days later they came to Capua.

 Note:
In the above example, *post*, which is usually a preposition followed by the accusative (e.g. **post merīdiem** (*after midday*)), is used adverbially.

The ablative also expresses 'time within which':

tribus diēbus Rōmam reueniam.
I shall return to Rome within three days.

Note that this use of the ablative developed into an alternative to the accusative expressing 'time how long'.

| Some Latin 'time' words and expressions

heri, here	yesterday
hodiē	today
crās	tomorrow

prīdiē	on the day before
posterō diē, postrīdiē	on the next day
abhinc[1]····▶	ago
interdiū	by day
intrā + *acc.*	within (**intrā trēs annōs** within three years)
māne	in the morning, early next day
mediā nocte	in the middle of the night, at midnight
merīdiē	at midday
multā nocte	late at night
multō diē	late in the day
noctū/nocte	at night
per + *acc.*	throughout (**per tōtum diem** throughout the whole day)
prīmā hōrā	at the first hour[2]····▶
prīmā lūce	at first light, at dawn
proximus, -a, -um	closest in time, last, next
proximā nocte	last night *or* the coming night (*depending on the context*).
quamdiū?	how long?
quotannīs	every year
quotīdiē, cotīdiē	every day
sōlis occāsū	at sunset
sōlis ortū	at sunrise
sub lūcem	towards daybreak
sub uesperum	towards evening
tertiīs uigiliīs	during the third watch[2]····▶
uesperī	in the evening

····▶ 1. This adverb is used with both the accusative and the ablative: **abhinc annōs trēs** and **abhinc annīs tribus** mean *three years ago*—**abhinc** is an adverb, not a preposition.

····▶ 2. The time of daylight was divided into twelve *hours* (**hōra, hōrae**, *f.*, *an hour*). Thus in summer the hours were longer than in winter. The time of night was divided in the same way, but in military language it was divided into four *watches* (**uigiliae, uigiliārum**, *f.pl.*).

For the date in Latin, see pp. 145–6.

| Place

- In Latin the 'place *to* which' is expressed by **in** or **ad** with the *accusative*:
  ad oppidum
  to the town
  in Graeciam
  to Greece

Note that **ad Graeciam nāuigāuī** means *I sailed to Greece* in the sense of
towards Greece, while **in Graeciam iī** means *I went to Greece* and actually set
foot there.

- The 'place *from* which' is expressed by **ā**, **ab**, **ē** or **ex** with the *ablative*:
  ex oppidō
  from the town
  ā flūmine
  from the river

- The 'place where' is expressed by **in** with the *ablative:*
  in oppidō
  in the town
  in Britanniā
  in Britain

However, if the place is a town, city, or small island (Rhodes is the largest
small island), the place name is usually put into the appropriate case *without* the preposition. The same applies to three common nouns, **domus, domī**
(or **domūs**), *f.* (*house, home*), **rūs, rūris,** *n.* (*country, countryside*), and **humus,
humī,** *f.* (*ground*).

Athēnās nāuigāuērunt.
They sailed to Athens.
Rōmā abiērunt.
They went away from Rome.
rūs Rōmā effūgī.
I fled to the country from Rome.

The *locative* case expresses place where, e.g. **Rōmae** means *at Rome*. For the formation of this case, see p. 18, n. 8.

☑ **Note:**

domī	at home
humī	on the ground
rūrī	in the country

| Latin 'place' words

ubi, ubi?	where, where?
hīc	here
ibi	there
illīc	there
ibīdem, ibidem	in the same place
utrimque	on both sides
quō, quō?	to where, to where?
hūc	to here
eō	to there
illūc	to there
eōdem	to the same place
usque	all the way (+ **ad** + *acc.*, right up to)
unde, unde?	from where, from where?
hinc	from here
inde	from there, then
illinc	from there
indidem	from the same place
undique	from everywhere
quā, quā?	by what route, by what route?
hāc	by this route
eā	by that route
illāc	by that route
alibī	elsewhere
nusquam	nowhere
ubīque	everywhere

| Space

The *accusative* is used to express distances and dimensions:

Arpīnum sexāgintā mīlia passuum ab urbe abest.
Arpinum is sixty miles away from the city.
flūmen uīgintī pedēs lātum trānsiērunt.
They crossed a river twenty feet wide.

| Practice sentences

Translate into English or Latin as appropriate:

1. **māter mea, prīmā hōrā profecta, sex hōrās ambulāuit et merīdiē Rōmam aduēnit.**
2. **Rōma trēdecim mīlia passuum ā marī distat.**
3. **labōribus urbānīs dēfessus, cōnsul rūs Rōmā rediit.**
4. **postrīdiē Brundisiō discessī ut in Graeciam aduenīrem.**
5. Where have you come from? Where are you going to? How long will you stay with us?
6. She was sick for the whole day and died at midnight.
7. Leave Rome and sail to Rhodes (Rhodus, Rhodi, *f.*) at once.
8. I shall visit you again within two years.

Participles

The girl <u>reading</u> the book.
A <u>rolling</u> stone gathers no moss.
The boy <u>about to read</u> the book.
Mother, <u>having read</u> the book.
It's silly to cry over <u>spilt</u> milk.

Participles are verbal adjectives, i.e. they are formed from verbs and so describe an action, but they are adjectives and so in Latin almost always agree with a noun or pronoun.

Present participles

Present participles end in **-ns** (**-āns** (first conjugation) or **-ēns** (all other verbs)). They can be formed from deponent verbs. They decline like *ingēns*, except that their ablative singular ends in **e** (*am*-**ante**), though the ending is **ī** when they are used in a purely adjectival sense, e.g. **ā uirō ambulantī** (*by the walking man*). Their genitive plural sometimes ends in **-tum** (*am*-**antum**) in poetry.

 Note:
   1 **sum** (*I am*) and **fīō** (*I become*) do not have present participles.
   2 The present participle of **eō** (I go) is **iēns, euntis**. (The nominative participle of uncompounded **eō** is very rare.)

The action described in the present participle always takes place at the same time as the action of the main verb. (Expressions using the words 'while' or 'during' are often used in English to convey this.)

cēnam edēns, puer laetus erat.
The boy was happy while eating the meal.

puerō ēsurientī cēnam dedī.
I gave a meal to the hungry boy.

exercitum proficīscentem hortātus est.
He encouraged the army while it was setting out.

Atalanta est celerrima puellārum currentium.
Atalanta is the fastest of the running girls.

☑ **Note:**
In its use of the present participle, English is often less precise than Latin in the matter of time.
<u>Getting</u> *into her chariot, Boudicca drove off aggressively.*
Latin could not use the present participle here since Boudicca got into her chariot *before* she drove off. Something like *postquam in currum cōnscendit* (= *after she had got into her chariot*) would be needed.

| Future participles

These are active in meaning: 'about to see', 'on the point of getting up', 'about to set out'. They are formed by adding **-ūrus, -a, -um** (declined like *bonus*) to the stem of the verb (in active verbs the supine without the final -**um**). They can be formed from deponents.
uīsūrus, surrēctūrus, profectūrus

Of what verbs are these the future participles? What do the participles mean?

Note the irregular future participle of *morior* (I die), **moritūrus**.

Rōmam relictūrus es?
Are you about to leave Rome?

omnia semper āctūra, nihil cōnficit.
Always on the point of doing everything, she finishes nothing.

locūtūrus eram cum tumultus ērūpit.
I was about to speak when a riot broke out.

☑ Note:
In poetry and later prose writers, the future participle can express purpose:
Maroboduus mīsit lēgātōs ad Tiberium ōrātūrōs auxilia.
(Tacitus, Annals, 2.46)
Maroboduus sent ambassadors to Tiberius to beg for help.

| Past participles

Past participles are formed by adding **-us**, **-a**, **-um** (declined like *bonus*) to the stem of the verb (the supine without the final *-um*).

All those formed from **active** verbs (the vast majority) are *passive* in meaning.

puellam cōnspectam salūtāuī.
Having caught sight of the girl, I greeted her.

cōnspectam is passive. It in fact means 'having been seen', *not* 'having seen'. Therefore if a Latin writer wishes to use a participle here, he has to say 'I greeted the having-been-seen girl.'

'Having been' is a useful aid in translating past participles, but it is unacceptable in English. The sentence above could be translated in a variety of ways, e.g.

I caught sight of the girl and greeted her.
After (when) I had caught sight of the girl, I greeted her.
Catching sight of the girl, I greeted her.
On (after) catching sight of the girl, I greeted her.

Rōmā expulsus, magnopere dolēbam.
Driven out of Rome (after *or* because I had been driven out of Rome), I was very distressed.

nautam ē nāue ēiectum in salūtem trāxī.
I dragged the sailor (who had been) flung out of his ship to safety.

puella 'amāta nōbīs quantum amābitur nūlla'. (Catullus, 8.5)
A girl beloved by us as much as no girl will ever be loved.

Deponent verbs (which are passive in form and active in meaning) have *active* past participles.

in urbem ingressa, ad forum accessī.
Having gone into the city (going into the city), I went to the forum.

prīmā lūce profectus, Rōmam sōlis occāsū aduēnī.
After setting out at dawn, I reached Rome at sunset.

☑ Note:

The past participles of deponent and semi-deponent verbs are often used to refer to actions which began before the action of the main verb *but* continue and overlap with the action of that verb.

Marcellum esse ratī, portās clausērunt.
Thinking it was Marcellus, they shut the gates.
They thought it was Marcellus both *before* and *during* the shutting of the gates.

| Ablative absolute

In all the examples in the first three sections of this chapter the participles have agreed with the subject or object of a verb or with a noun or a pronoun which forms some other part of the clause it belongs to, as in this sentence:

Cicerō epistulam lēctam Tīrōnī iuxtā sedentī trādidit.
Cicero read the letter and handed it over to Tiro who was sitting nearby.
Literally: Cicero handed over the having-been-read letter to Tiro sitting nearby.

Often, however, the participial phrase (i.e. the noun + the participle) is independent of the structure of the rest of the sentence, e.g.

Caesar, hīs dictīs, mīlitēs dīmīsit.
After saying these things, Caesar dismissed the soldiers.
Literally: Caesar, these things having been said, dismissed the soldiers.

dictīs agrees with *hīs*, which is not the subject or object of the main verb and is independent of the clause in which it sits. The technical term for this is 'absolute' (= loosed *or* freed). In phrases such as this, both noun and participle are in the ablative case.

This construction does not go very naturally into English, and, while it is helpful for the translator to use 'having been' to begin with, it is important to move on to more idiomatic translations.

cēnā parātā, coquus quiēscēbat.
When dinner was ready (literally, dinner having been prepared), the cook had a rest.

Cicerōne locūtō, Tīrō gaudēbat.
After Cicero had spoken (literally, Cicero having spoken), Tiro was delighted.

Horātiō in Acadēmīā studente, Brūtus Athēnās aduēnit.
(While) Horace (was) studying in the Academy, Brutus arrived at Athens.

••••▶ Note

1 Remember that the ablative singular of the present participle, when it is used as a participle, ends in -e.

2 Remember that uncompounded **sum** has no present participle. In the following phrases, this non-existent present participle is understood:

mē (tē, etc.) inuītō
against my (your, etc.) will

tē (Caesare, etc.) duce
under your (Caesar's, etc.) leadership

mē (tē, etc.) auctōre
at my (your, etc.) suggestion

Cicerōne cōnsule
when Cicero was consul, in the consulship of Cicero.

Note also

mē praesente, mē absente
in my presence, in my absence

| Practice sentences

Translate into English or Latin as appropriate:

1. haec dīxit moriēns.
2. haec scrībēns maximē dolēbam.
3. illī ad mortem euntī succurrī.
4. urbem oppugnātūrus cōnstitit.
5. amīcus adest auxilium mihi lātūrus.
6. hoc somnium ueritus, Caesar cōnstituit ā cūriā abesse.
7. puellīs uīsīs, puerī multō laetiōrēs factī sunt.
8. liber ā tē datus mihi magnopere placuit.
9. serpentem in herbā cēlātam Eurydicē nōn uīdit.
10. Caesare duce, exercitus Rōmānus Britannōs dēbellāuit.
11. While walking in the town I saw my sister.
12. I saw my sister walking in the town.
13. When on the point of setting out, I embraced my husband lovingly.
14. I thanked (gratias ago + *dative*) the young man (who was) about to help me.
15. Leaving (*use* relinquō) the town I walked happily (*use* laetus) through the fields.
16. She captured the city and burnt it (*use a participle for* 'captured').
17. He threw away the book after he had read it (*use a participle for* 'after he had read').
18. After setting out early from the city, I reached the harbour at mid-day.
19. The general called his soldiers together and left the camp (*use a participle*).
20. After my friend's departure, I was very unhappy (egredior = *I depart*).

Indirect statement

Direct speech	Indirect speech
I am reading the book.	I said <u>I was reading the book</u>.
I have read the book.	I knew that <u>I had read the book</u>.
I shall read the book.	I promised that <u>I would read the book</u>.

An **indirect statement** comes after a verb in which the voice, ears, eyes, or mind is used (e.g. say, hear, discover, see, observe, know, think), followed by 'that', or with 'that' understood, e.g.

I think that I am ill. I think I am ill.

It can be seen from the examples above that in English the words of direct speech are usually changed when they are converted into indirect speech. The Latin words change too, but in a different way.

The subject of the clause in indirect speech is in the *accusative*, and it must not be left out (though see note 6 below). The verb is in the *infinitive* and the infinitive is in *the tense of the words actually spoken or thought*. The infinitive exists in three tenses, present, future, and perfect.

This construction is often called 'the accusative and infinitive', and it is found in good English usage, e.g.

I believe him to be a fool.

Active

dīxī mē librum legere. (same time)
I said I was reading the book.

dīxī mē librum lēctūrum esse. (later time)
I said that I would read the book.

dīxī mē librum lēgisse. (earlier time)
I said I had read the book.

Passive

dīxī librum ā mē legī.
I said that the book was being read by me.

prōmīsī librum ā mē lēctum īrī.
I promised that the book would be read by me.

scīuī librum ā mē lēctum esse.
I knew that the book had been read by me.

···▶ **Note**

1 The reflexives **sē** and **suus** refer back to the subject of the verb which introduces the indirect statement.

Marcus scīuit sē suum librum eī dedisse.
Marcus knew that he (Marcus) had given his (own) book to him (or her, certainly to someone else).

2 In the infinitives which include participles (future active–*lēctūrus esse*, perfect passive–*lēctus esse*), the participle agrees with the *accusative* subject of the infinitive.

uxor mea dīcit sē Bāiās aditūram esse.
My wife says that she will go to Baiae.

The future passive infinitive, however, which is very rare, never changes (supine plus *īrī*). Latin prefers *fore ut* (it will be (come about) that) followed by the subjunctive:

spērō fore ut dēleātur Carthāgō.
I hope that Carthage will be destroyed.

3 'Say ... not' is negō (1). *dīcō* is only followed by *nōn* when a single word is negatived.

marītus negāuit sē Rōmae mānsūrum esse.
The husband said that he would not stay at Rome.

pater dīxit sē nōn mihi sed Marcō librum dedisse.
Father said that he had given the book not to me but to Marcus.

Note the following:

negō quemquam	I say that no one
negō quicquam	I say that nothing
negō ūllum ...	I say that no . . .
negō . . . umquam	I say that . . . never
negō . . . usquam	I say that . . . nowhere

4 Verbs meaning 'hope', 'promise', and 'threaten' are usually followed in English by the word 'to', i.e. by the infinitive. In Latin they are followed by the accusative and infinitive construction, and the infinitive is usually future.

minātus est sē mē necātūrum esse.
He threatened to kill me. *Literally*: He threatened that he would kill me.

But hopes and promises *can* refer to the present or past—in which case the present or perfect infinitive is used.

spērō Herculem leōnem occīdisse.
I hope that Hercules has killed the lion.

5 Subordinate clauses in indirect statement have their verbs in the subjunctive, the tense to be determined by the sequence of tenses (see pp. 86–7) established by the main verb.

dīcit sē librum lēgisse quem sibi dederim.
He says that he has read the book which I gave him.

iūrāuit sē librum lēctūrum esse quem scrīpsissem.
He swore that he would read the book which I had written.

mē certiōrem fēcit sē uenīre ad oppidum ubi habitārem.
He informed me that he was on his way to the town where I was living.

6 Indirect statement can continue from one main clause to another. The main verb does not need to be repeated as long as its subject remains unchanged. Also, if the subject of the second or subsequent infinitives is the same as that of the first infinitive, it does not have to be repeated.

dīxit sē sine marītō Bāiās adiisse; inter plūrimōs lautissimōs quī sē eō congregāuissent iūcundē uīuere; in animō habēre diū in eō locō manēre.
She said that she had gone to Baiae without her husband; (she went on to say that she) was having a pleasant time among the very many highly fashionable people who had gathered there; (she added that) she planned to stay in that place for a long time.

7 There are two future infinitives of *sum*, **futūrus esse** and **fore**.

8 **cōnstituō** (I decide) is followed by a present infinitive when the subject of the dependent verb is the same as the subject of *cōnstituō*.

cōnstituī urbem relinquere.
I decided to leave the city.

9 Verbs which introduce indirect statement in fact cover a much wider ground than mere statement, as can be seen from the following (by no means exhaustive) list, which should be learnt:

arbitror (1)	I think
audiō (4)	I hear
(aliquem) certiōrem faciō, facere, fēcī, factum	I inform (someone)
cognōscō, cognōscere, cognōuī, cognitum	I get to know, discover
cōnstat (inter omnēs)	it is common knowledge
crēdō, crēdere, crēdidī, crēditum	I believe
dīcō, dīcere, dīxī, dictum	I say
discō, discere, didicī,—	I learn
exīstimō (1)	I think
ferunt	men say
ignōrō (1)	I am unaware
intellegō, intellegere, intellēxī, intellēctum	I understand (*like* legō)
iūrō (1)	I swear
meminī, meminisse	I remember
minor (1)	I threaten
nārrō (1)	I tell, relate
negō (1)	I say . . . not

nōsco, nōscere, nōuī, nōtum	I get to know, find out
nūntiō (1)	I announce
polliceor (2)	I promise
prō certō habeō (2)	I am certain
prōmittō, prōmittere, prōmīsī, prōmissum	I promise (*like* mittō)
putō (1)	I think
respondeō, respondēre, respondī, respōnsum	I reply
sciō (4)	I know
nesciō (4)	I do not know (*like* sciō)
scrībō, scrībere, scrīpsī, scrīptum	I write
sentiō, sentīre, sēnsī, sēnsum	I perceive, feel
spērō (1)	I hope
uideō, uidēre, uīdī, uīsum	I see

| Practice sentences

Translate into English or Latin as appropriate:

1. frātrem tuum fortem esse intellegō.
2. puella mihi dīxit sē dōnō meō dēlectātam esse.
3. puer mē certiōrem fēcit puellam dōnum suum nōndum accēpisse.
4. negāuī mē ante aduentum tuum abitūrum esse.
5. prōmittō mē carmina recitātūrum esse quae Horātius mihi mīserit.
6. explōrātor Caesarī nūntiāuit hostēs iam nōn procul abesse; maximum igitur perīculum Rōmānīs imminēre.
7. I think that she is much cleverer than he is.
8. Marcus said that his friend would give him back the book which he had lent (trado) him.
9. He says that the city will never be captured.
10. I hope to see you soon and I promise to bring you a present.
11. I realized that he was no longer friendly to me, and (realized) that he was unwilling to speak to me.
12. The senators were informed that the women were picketing (obsideo) the streets which led to the senate house.

Sequence of tenses

In Latin, the tense of the subjunctive used in a subordinate clause is affected by the tense of the main verb. This process occurs in English too.

> I am helping you so that you <u>can/may</u> get better.
> I was helping you so that you <u>could/might</u> get better.

We call this process 'sequence of tenses' and it falls into two divisions, which we call *primary* (mainly present and future tenses) and *historic* or *secondary* (past tenses).

Primary sequence

Tense of verb in main clause	*Tense of subjunctive in subordinate clause*
present imperative future 'perfect with *have*'[1] ····▸ future perfect	present (referring to the present or the future) perfect (referring to the past)

····▸ 1. The 'perfect with *have*' is a shorthand expression for a perfect which tells us about a present state, e.g. cognōuī (I [have got to] know), intellēxī (I [have understood =] understand), and uēnistis (you [have come =] are present).

Historic sequence

Tense of verb in main clause	*Tense of subjunctive in subordinate clause*
imperfect 'perfect without *have*' (aorist) pluperfect	imperfect (referring to the same time or a later time) pluperfect (referring to something that has already happened)

While some would consider it pedantry, many good judges would argue that it is desirable to preserve the distinction between 'may' and 'might' according to sequence of tenses in English as well as Latin. For example:

I am speaking slowly in the hope that you <u>may</u> understand me.
The teacher spoke slowly in the hope that his students <u>might</u> understand him.

Direct and indirect command

Direct command

1 | Second person commands

Do this. Don't do that.

- Positive direct commands in the second person are expressed in Latin by the imperative. **and don't** (e.g. do this *and don't* do that) = neque/nec.
- Negative direct commands are expressed by *nōlī* (singular) and *nōlīte* (plural) (= refuse to, be unwilling to) followed by the present infinitive. *nē* + present or perfect subjunctive can be used. **and don't** = neu/nēue + *present* subjunctive.

> **amā mē fidēliter.**
> Love me faithfully.

> **ī, sequere Italiam.**
> Go, make for Italy. (Virgil, Dido to Aeneas, *Aeneid*, 4.381)

> **audī mē nec abī.**
> Listen to me and don't go away.

> **nōlīte spēluncās intrāre.**
> Don't go into the caves.

> **nē fēcerīs quod timēs.**
> Don't do something you're frightened of.

> **illud nē fēcerīs nēue dīxerīs.**
> Do not do or say that.

☑ **Note:**
1 In negative direct commands in verse, *nē* can be followed by the imperative:
  nē fuge mē.   Don't run away from me.
(Ovid, Jupiter to a prospective rape victim, *Metamorphoses*, 1.597)
2 The singular imperatives of *dīcō, dūcō, ferō, faciō* are dīc, dūc, fer, fac.

| First and third person commands

Let's go to see her. Let them hate me.

● Commands in the first and third person are expressed by the present subjunctive. Negative *nē*. **and not** = *neu/nēue*.

  amet.
  Let him love.
  exeat nēue plūra dīcat.
  Let him go out and say no more.
  gaudeāmus.
  Let us rejoice.

| Indirect command

He ordered me to go away.
He asked me to do this.

With two exceptions, all words of commanding and forbidding are followed by the same construction. This is **ut** or **nē** + the present or imperfect subjunctive (depending on sequence of tenses—see pp. 86–7). [The construction is the same as the purpose clause: see pp. 96–8.]

····▶ **Note**

1 Latin uses this construction not just for 'order to' or 'tell to', or 'decree that' but for less decisive and authoritative words too, e.g. 'advise to', 'ask to', 'beg to', 'pray to', 'encourage to', 'warn to', 'persuade to'. iubeō (see note 2) is often more like 'ask to' than 'order to' in meaning.

2 Be careful to use **ut** or **nē** plus the subjunctive. (English tends to invite an infinitive.) The two exceptions are **iubeō, iubēre, iussī, iussum** = I order, and its converse **uetō, uetāre, uetuī, uetitum** = I order . . . not, I forbid. Both are followed by an accusative and infinitive. **iubeō** cannot be followed by **nōn** (except where *nōn* negatives a single word: **iubeō tē nōn hunc sed illum sequī** (*I order you to follow not this man but that one*)): **uetō** (or **imperō nē**) must be used instead.

> **tibi imperō ut hoc faciās.**
> I tell you to (*literally*, that you should) do this.

> **imperātor suīs imperāuit nē prōgrederentur.**
> The general ordered his men not to (*literally*, that they should not) advance.

> **Vbiī Caesarem ōrant ut sibi parcat.**
> The Ubii beg Caesar to (*literally*, that he should) spare them.

> **hoc nē faciās admoneō.**
> I advise you not to do this.

> **mē iussit hoc facere.**
> He ordered me to do this.

> **mē uetuit abīre.**
> He told me not (forbade me) to go away. ····▶

····▶ The English word 'tell' can often mean 'order' (see p. 141).

---

3 The reflexives *sē* and *suus* refer back to the subject of the verb which introduces the indirect command.

The following verbs should be learnt:

ē-dīcō, -dīcere, -dīxī, -dictum	I proclaim, decree
flagitō (1)	I demand
hortor (1) **/ adhortor** (1)	I encourage
imperō (1) + dat.	I order
iubeō, iubēre, iussī, iussum + infinitive	I order
moneō (2) **/ admoneō** (2)	I advise, warn
obsecrō (1)	I beseech
ōrō (1)	I beg
petō, petere, petīuī, petītum	I seek, ask
poscō, poscere, poposcī,–	I demand
postulō (1)	I demand, direct
prae-cipiō, -cipere, -cēpī, -ceptum + dat.	I order
prae-dīcō, -dīcere, -dīxī, -dictum + dat. (like **dīcō**)	I make known
precor (1)	I pray
rogō (1)	I ask

suādeō / per-suādeō, -suādēre, -suāsī, -suāsum + dat.   I urge, persuade
uetō, uetāre, uetuī, uetitum + infinitive   I forbid, order not

| Practice sentences

Translate into English or Latin as appropriate:

1. uenī hūc et dīc mihi id quod uīs.
2. nē ab urbe fugiat. occīde eum.
3. suīs imperāuit ut propius accēderent.
4. patrī meō persuāsī ut Rōmam uenīret.
5. Pompēius suīs praedīxerat ut Caesaris impetum exciperent nēue timērent.
6. I say, 'Do this!' and he does it.
7, 8. I ordered the girl to do this. (*Express this in two different ways.*)
9. I told the young man not to do this. (*Use* ueto.)
10. He was persuading me to leave my husband.
11. Leave the town and do not return.
12. I encouraged my teacher to work harder.

Direct and indirect questions

Direct questions

What are you doing?
When will you do that?
You can't be thinking of doing that, can you?

Latin has two ways of asking direct questions. In both of them the verb is regularly in the indicative.

- If the question is introduced by a word that asks a question (e.g. *who? when? why?*, etc.), the word used will be one of the following:

quis? quid?	who? what?
quī, quae, quod?	which? what? (adjective of above)
quālis, quālis, quāle	what sort of?
uter, utra, utrum?	which (of two)?
quam?	how? (to what degree?) (with adjective or adverb)
quōmodo? quemadmodum?	how? (in what way?)
quantus, quanta, quantum?	how great?
quot? (indeclinable)	how many?
quotiēns? quotiēs?	how often?
quamdiū?	how long? (*of time*)
cūr? quārē? quam ob rem? quid?	why?
quandō?	when?
ubi? quā?	where?
quō?	where to? whither?
unde?	from where? whence?

quid dīcis?
What are you saying?
quot līberōs habet rēgīna?
How many children does the queen have?

quō uādis, domine?
Where are you going to, master?

- If the question is not introduced by one of the above words which asks a question, see which of the following applies in the Latin:

1 If the answer to the question could be *yes* **or** *no*, you may find **-ne** added to the first word (which should be the emphatic word). However, just as in English, a question can be indicated by the sense or the context, without the reinforcement of **-ne**.

2 If the questioner is expecting the answer *yes*, the question will begin with **nōnne**.

Surely you saw him?
You did want to come to my grammar class, didn't you?

3 If the questioner is expecting the answer *no*, the question will begin with **num**.

You didn't see him, did you?
Surely you don't enjoy blood sports?

4 If there is a double question, you will probably find **utrum . . . an** or **-ne** (see 1) **. . . an**. Negative **utrum . . . annōn/necne**.

Are you laughing at him or at me?
Are you going to do this work or not?

You need not find a translation for **utrum** in direct questions. It simply informs you that a second half to the question is coming up.

5 an can introduce a question containing the notion of surprise or indignation:

an nescīs quae sit haec rēs? (Plautus, Pseudolus, 1161)
Can you really be unaware what this business is about?

mēne fugis?
Is it me you are running away from?
(Virgil, Dido to Aeneas, Aeneid, 4.314)

nōnne meministī?
You do remember, don't you?

num huius oblīta es?
Surely you haven't forgotten him/her/this?

seruīne estis an līberī?
Are you slaves or free men?

utrum eum uīdistī annōn?
Did you see him or not?

Indirect questions

A verb in which the voice, eyes, ears, or mind is used (e.g. ask, observe, hear, deduce) followed by a word which asks a question (*who? when? why?, etc.*) is followed by a *question word plus the subjunctive*. The question words are the same as for direct questions. But note that 'if', 'whether' = **num** or **an** (not **sī**). **This is an important distinction.** After *num*, **quis, quid** is used for 'anyone', 'anything'.

The tense of the subjunctive corresponds to the English, but sequence of tenses (see pp. 86–70) is, of course, observed:

	Primary	*Historic*
Present	**scit quid agam.**	**scīuit quid agerem.**
	He knows what I am doing.	He knew what I was doing.
Past	**scit quid ēgerim** (perf. subj.)	**scīuit quid ēgissem** (pluperf. subj.)
	He knows what I did.	He knew what I had done.
Future	**scit quid āctūrus sim.**	**scīuit quid āctūrus essem**
	He knows what I am going to do (shall do).	He knew what I was going to do (would do).

There is no future subjunctive in Latin. For this construction the language has to use a future participle together with the present or imperfect subjunctive of **sum** (whichever the sequence calls for).

> **minimī meā interest utrum rūrī mānsūrus sīs an Rōmam aduentūrus sīs.**
> It makes very little difference to me whether you stay in the country or come to Rome.

☑ **Note:**
necne (not **annōn**) is used to mean 'or not' in indirect questions.

Practice sentences

Translate into English or Latin as appropriate:

1. **quot librōs habet Atticus?**
2. **num tibi sum causa dolōris?**
3. **uīuitne pater?**

4. **quaerunt utrum dī sint necne.**
5. **quis scit quālia tempora reī pūblicae futūra sint?**
6. What do you think about the weather?
7. Where are you now? Where did you set out from, and where are you going to?
8. I asked him what he now had in mind.
9. I told him what I was about to ask the king.
10. I am asking myself whether you are foolish or not.
11. Surely no one can be so stupid?

Purpose clauses

I went to Rome	to see	
	in order to see	the emperor.
	so as to see	

To express purpose Latin uses **ut** (= in order that) or, in the negative, **nē** (= in order that . . . not, lest, in case, to prevent) followed by the *present* or *imperfect* subjunctive depending on the sequence of tenses.

In this construction the sequence of tenses (see pp. 86–7) means that if the verb in the main clause is a present, imperative, future, or perfect with *have*, the verb in the **ut/nē** clause will be in the *present* subjunctive. If the verb in the main clause is in a *past* tense (imperfect, 'perfect without *have*', pluperfect), the verb in the **ut/nē** clause will be in the *imperfect* subjunctive.

Rōmam accēdō ut prīncipem uideam.

I am going to Rome	so that I may see the emperor,
	to see the emperor, etc.

Rōmam adiī ut prīncipem uidērem.

I went to Rome	so that I *might* see the emperor,
	in order to see the emperor, etc.

••••➤ Note

1 In English, *may* and *might* are often equivalents of the Latin present and imperfect subjunctives respectively.

2 English often uses the infinitive to express purpose. Such an infinitive is not very common in classical Latin literature. **ut** . . . **nōn** must *never* be used in this construction (except when **nōn** negates a single word). Remember that the negative of **ut** is **nē**.

Rōmā excessit nē Antōnium uidēret.
He left Rome in order not to see Antony.

Note also:

nē quis, quis, quid	in order that nobody . . . , in case anybody . . . , etc.
nē ūllus, ūlla, ūllum	so that no . . . (stronger than **nē quis**)
nē umquam, nē quandō	so that . . . never . . .
nē usquam, nēcubi	so that . . . nowhere . . .

3 **neu** or **nēue** (and not) introduces a second purpose clause if it is negative.

Rōmā excessit nē Antōnium uidēret neu cōntiōnem audīret.

He left Rome in order to avoid seeing Antony and hearing his speech (*literally*, and so as not to hear . . .).

4 When the purpose clause contains a comparative adjective or adverb, **quō** is used instead of **ut**.

cucurrī quō celerius eō aduenīrem.

I ran so as to get there faster.

5 The relative pronoun (**quī, quae, quod**) is used with the subjunctive to express purpose.

lēgātōs mīsit quī pācem peterent.

He sent ambassadors to seek peace (*literally*, who might seek . . .).

Rōmānī arma rapiunt quibus urbem suam dēfendant.

The Romans seize their arms in order to defend their city (literally, with which they may defend . . .).

The relative pronoun is regularly used in place of **ut** after verbs of giving, sending, and choosing, if the subject of the main clause is the same as the subject of the purpose clause.

6 **sē** or **suus** in a purpose clause is likely to refer back to the subject of the main clause. See the last example.

7 Note the following words and phrases which can occur in main clauses and serve as a kind of *signpost* for a purpose clause:

idcircō	for this reason
ideō	for this reason
eō	for this/that purpose
proptereā	on this account
eō cōnsiliō	with this/that intention
eā causā	for this/that reason
eā rē	for this/that reason

Cicerō eō cōnsiliō locūtus est ut Antōnium damnāret.

Cicero spoke with the intention of condemning Antony.

8 The supine (ending **-um**) can be used to express purpose after verbs of motion and verbs implying motion.

lēgātōs mīsit pācem petītum.

He sent ambassadors to seek peace.

Note **cubitum eō** = I go to bed: **cubitum** is the supine of **cubō** (**cubō, cubāre, cubuī, cubitum,** I lie down, I lie asleep). Thus **cubitum eō** literally means 'I go to lie down'.

9 For the use of the *future participle* and the *gerund and gerundive* to express purpose, see pp. 78 and 110 respectively.

10 utī is a variant spelling of **ut** and must be distinguished from **ūtī**, the present infinitive of the verb **ūtor** (= I use).

11 Purpose clauses are often called final clauses (from **fīnis** = end), referring to the *end* or purpose in view.

| Practice sentences

Translate into English or Latin as appropriate:

1. **puellae currunt ut ad fontem ueniant.**
2. **cauē nē quis molestus tibi approprinquet.**
3. **lentius loquere quō tē facilius intellegam.**
4. **haec uerba idcircō locūtus sum ut hanc rem haud dubiē intellegerēs.**
5. **semper habē Pyladēn aliquem quī cūret Orestēn.** (Ovid, Remedia Amoris, 589. Pylades was a close and protective friend of Orestes. 'Pyladēn' and 'Orestēn' are Greek accusatives.)
6. **ut amēris, amābilis estō** (= be). (Ovid, Ars Amatoria, 2.107)

7, 8, Express in *three* different ways:
& 9. Caesar sent out scouts to find the enemy's camp.

10. We set out at dawn so that we could reach home more quickly.
11. I went to bed in order to have a good rest (= rest well).
12. Leave the city in case any enemy (inimicus) sees you anywhere and does not spare you.

Result clauses

I ran so fast that I collapsed.
Matilda told such dreadful lies, she made you gasp and stretch your
 eyes.

Result is expressed in Latin by **ut** (= so that, so as to) or **ut nōn** (so that ...
not) plus the subjunctive. The subjunctive is in the natural tense (i.e. the
tense is dictated by the sense). It is extremely likely to be the present or
imperfect subjunctive depending on sequence of tenses. (see pp. 86–7)

● The present subjunctive in historic sequence stresses the 'actuality' of
 the result: it is *now* true. Compare the following:

　　tot uulnera accēpit ut moriātur.
　　He received so many wounds that he is (now) dying.

　　tot uulnera accēpit ut morerētur.
　　He received so many wounds that he was dying.

　　tot uulnera accēpit ut mortuus sit.
　　He received so many wounds that he died. (He has received so
　　　many wounds that he is dead.)

The perfect subjunctive stresses the completion of the result.

● If a future subjunctive is needed, the future participle plus **sim** or **essem**
 (according to sequence of tenses) is used.

　　tam dīligenter labōrāmus ut crās in lectō mānsūrī simus.
　　We are working so hard that we shall stay in bed tomorrow.

••••▶ Note

1　This construction is very frequently *signposted* by one of the following words:

tālis, tālis, tāle	such, of such a kind
tantus, tanta, tantum	so great, so large
tot (indeclinable)	so many
totiēns, totiēs	so often, so many times
tam (with adjectives or adverbs)	so ...
adeō (with verbs)	so much, to such an extent
ita	so (in such a way)
sīc	so (in such a way)

Note that **tālis** is not used with another adjective. The Latin for 'such a brave man' is **uir tam fortis**.

2 In result clauses the reflexives **sē** and **suus** refer to the subject of the **ut/ut nōn** clause. So in the following sentence, **eum** is used, not **sē**.

tam fācundus erat Pompēius ut omnēs eum laudārent.
Pompeius was so eloquent that everyone used to praise him.

3 Remember that the negative of **ut** in this construction is **ut nōn** (not **nē**). When there is a second result clause and it is negative, Latin uses **nec** or **neque** (not **nēue**).

tam clārē Mārcum de illīs rēbus certiōrem fēcit ut omnia intellegeret neque iam esset ignārus.
So clearly did he inform Marcus about these things that he understood everything and was no longer in ignorance.

Note also:

ut nēmō	that nobody ...
ut nihil	that nothing ...
ut nūllus	that no ...
ut numquam	that never ...
ut nusquam	that nowhere ...

4 The relative with the subjunctive can be used to express result.

nōn tam stulta est Līuia quae mendācibus crēdat.
Livia is not so stupid as to trust liars. (Her stupidity is not so great that it leads to the result of her trusting liars (**quae = ut ea**).)

5 Note the idioms

sunt quī + subjunctive
there are some people who ...

is sum quī + subjunctive
I am the type of person who ...

sunt quī Graecōs meliōrēs quam Rōmānōs habeant.
There are people who consider Greeks superior to Romans.

ea est quae pauperēs semper cūret.
She is the sort of woman who is always looking after the poor.

We call this use of the subjunctive *generic* (from Latin **genus** (type, kind)) because it is used to convey the result of people being the 'types' they are.

6 **quam quī** (or **quam ut**) is used after a comparative in such sentences as

fortior est quam quī (ut) effugiat.
He is too brave to run away.
Literally, He is braver than the sort of man who runs away *or* He is too brave for the result to be that he runs away.

7 Note **dignus/indignus sum quī** + subjunctive = I am worthy/ unworthy to . . ., I deserve to . . ., I do not deserve to . . .

digna est quae morte pūniātur.
She deserves to be punished by death.
Literally, She is worthy so that (as a result) she should be punished by death.

8 Result clauses are also known as consecutive (i.e. consequence) clauses because the result clause *follows on* from (i.e. is a consequence of) the main clause.

| Practice sentences

Translate into English or Latin as appropriate:

1. **adeō terrēbar ut nihil facere possem.**
2. **ita carmina mea recitāuī ut omnēs dēlectārentur.**
3. **tam fortis est Herculēs ut omnia perīcula superātūrus sit.**
4. **nōn is sum quī ab inceptīs dēterrear.**
5. **Siciliam ita uastāuit ut restituī nūllō modō possit.**
6. **tanta uīs probitātis est, ut eam in hoste etiam dīligāmus.** (Cicero, de amicitia, 29)
7. He fled so fast that I couldn't catch him.
8. He deserves to be hanged.
9. There are some people who believe the orator's words.
10. I was so seriously beaten that I collapsed.
11. Who is so foolish as to believe you?
12. I am not the type to chase girls.

Verbs of fearing

I am afraid to do this.
I fear that the enemy will soon arrive.

Where English uses an infinitive after a verb of fearing, as in the first of these sentences, Latin also uses the infinitive.

timeō hoc facere.
I am afraid to do this.

Where in English the word 'that' follows (or is implied by) the verb of fearing, as in the following sentences, Latin uses **nē** + subjunctive.

timeō nē hostēs mox adveniant.
I am afraid (that) the enemy may soon arrive.

timeō nē mē prōdiderīs.
I am afraid (that) you have betrayed me.

The negative **nē** is logical since the person fearing hopes that the thing he or she fears will *not* happen. Old-fashioned English uses the negative word *lest* here:

I am afraid <u>lest</u> you (may) have betrayed me.

If you are working from English into Latin and find a clause of fearing that is *not* expressed in one of the above ways, you should re-cast it before translating, using 'that' or 'lest'.

He was afraid of being found.
Re-cast: He was afraid that he might be found.

timēbat nē inuenīrētur.

The tense of the subjunctive is determined by the sequence of tenses (see pp. 86–7). Note that the present subjunctive can refer to the future in primary sequence and the imperfect subjunctive can refer to the future in historic sequence. (The future participle + **sim/essem** is generally *not* used after verbs of fearing.)

uereor nē illa me uideat.
I am afraid that she will see me.

metuēbam nē illa mē uidēret.
I was afraid that she would see me.

The *negative* of **nē** is **nē … nōn** (or **nē numquam**, etc.) or **ut** (the latter never being used when the main verb is negative).

timuī nē mihi auxilium nōn ferrēs.
I was frightened that you would not bring me help.

Clauses of fearing are introduced by such words as:

timeō (2)	I fear, I am afraid
metuō, metuere, metuī, metūtum	I fear, I am afraid
paueō, pauēre, pāuī, —	I am frightened, terrified
uereor (2)	I fear, I am afraid
ueritus, uerita, ueritum	fearing
timor, timōris, *m.*	fear
metus, metūs, *m.*	fear
perīculum, perīculī, *n.*	danger

sē or **suus** in the fearing clause refers back to the subject of the main verb:

Cicerō timuit nē fūrēs mēnsam suam pretiōsam abriperent.
Cicero was afraid that thieves might steal his valuable table.

| Practice sentences

Translate into English or Latin as appropriate:

1. **timuī ex urbe in agrōs abīre.**
2. **imperātor metuit nē hostēs exercitum suum oppugnārent.**
3. **ueritus nē amīcam suam nōn uidēret, ad urbem ānxius properābat.**
4. **perīculum est nē soror tua sērius adueniat.**
5. **uereor nē dum dēfendam meōs, non parcam tuīs.** (Cicero, ad Atticum, 1.17.3)
6. She was afraid that the house might fall down.
7. I fear that she does not love your brother.
8. Fearing that I might offend you, I did not talk about your poetry.
9. Ulysses (Ulixes) was afraid that he would never see his home again.
10. I am afraid that I have killed your best friend.

Impersonal verbs

It rains.
It pours.
It's snowing.
It's thundering.

In English, impersonal verbs (i.e. verbs with *it* used as a sort of empty or dummy subject) are frequently used of the weather. They are used in other contexts, for example, *It upsets me that* . . ., though far less frequently. In Latin they fall into the following categories:

1 Weather verbs: **tonat** it thunders; **ningit** it snows; **pluit** it rains; **aduesperāscit** it is drawing towards evening.

2(a) impersonal verbs with a dative of the person and an infinitive:

dīcere mihi libet.
It pleases me to speak, I wish to speak.

dīcere mihi licet.
It is allowed to me to speak, i.e. I may speak.

dīcere mihi placet.
It pleases me to speak, I like speaking, I decide to speak.

dīcere mihi uidētur.
It seems a good idea to me to speak, I decide to speak.

All these verbs are in the 2nd conjugation.

2(b) impersonal verbs used with an accusative of the person and an infinitive:

dīcere mē decet.
It is fitting for me to speak.

dīcere mē oportuit.
It was my duty to speak (in old-fashioned English, It behoved me to speak).

dīcere mē iuuat.
It pleases me to speak, I like speaking.

decet and **oportet** are 2nd conjugation, **iuuat** is 1st.

3 Impersonal verbs of feeling: the person who feels is in the *accusative*; the cause of the feeling is in the *genitive*.

mē miseret rēgīnae.
I am sorry for (I pity) the queen.

mē paenitet dictōrum.
I am sorry for (I repent) my words.

mē piget studiōrum.
I am repelled by my studies. (in old-fashioned English, it irks ...)

mē pudēbat factōrum.
I was ashamed of my deeds.

mē taedet grammaticae.
I am tired of grammar. (cf. it wearies me)

All these verbs are 2nd conjugation. They can be used with the infinitive:

mē paenituit tot mala dē tē dīxisse.
I was sorry to have said so many bad things about you.

puellās lūdere pudet.
The girls are ashamed to play.

☑ **Note:**

1 meā (tuā, suā, nostrā, uestrā) interest
it is important to me (you, him, her, us, you*)*
meā (tuā, suā, nostrā, uestrā) rēfert
it concerns me (you, him, her, us, you)

With both *interes*t and *rēfert*, when one of the above pronominal adjectives is not used, the person or thing concerned is in the genitive.

2 necesse est + infinitive *or* subjunctive = *it is necessary*
3 accidit ut + subjunctive = *it happens that*

| **Practice sentences**

Translate into English or Latin as appropriate:

1 **imperātōrem miseret captīuōrum. licēbit eī illōs līberāre?**
2 **ōrātōrem amīcōs suōs dēfendere oportet, sed prō tālī dīcere mē magnopere puduit.**

3 **accidit ut ōrātiōnum meārum semper mē paeniteat.**
4 **ningit, sed uidētur mihi proficīscī.**
5 It is important for me to reach Capua.
6 Evening is approaching. Will the girls be allowed to come to my house?
7 It is fitting for good men to die for their fatherland.
8 I decided (*use an impersonal verb*) to run away from the battle.

| The impersonal use of the passive

I killed the king	They fought fiercely.
The king was killed.	There was fierce fighting.

In Latin, if a verb is used transitively (i.e. with an accusative object), it can be put in the passive by making what was the accusative object the new nominative subject.

rēgem interfēcī. rēx ā mē interfectus est.

However, this is not possible when a verb either is intransitive or is used intransitively.

ācriter pugnāuērunt.

This can only be rendered *impersonally* in the passive. The subject becomes *it*, i.e. the third person singular in the neuter.

ācriter pugnātum est.

This impersonal passive is especially common with verbs of motion.

prīmā lūce profectī sumus. merīdiē ad lacum peruentum est.
We set out at dawn. At midday we came (*literally*, it was come) to the lake.

undique concurritur.
People run together from every direction. *Literally*, It is run together from every direction

sīc ītur ad astra.
That (*i.e.* fame) is the way to the stars. *Literally*, Thus it is gone to the stars.

Verbs which are followed by the dative are also technically intransitive and so in the passive these too can only be used impersonally. (It is impossible to make the dative object of the active verb the nominative subject of the passive verb.)

lēgibus pārēmus. (active)
We obey the laws.

lēgibus ā nōbīs pārētur.
The laws are obeyed by us. *Literally*, There is obeying/obedience to the laws by us.

captīuīs parcētur.
The prisoners will be spared. *Literally*, There will be sparing to the prisoners.

cōnsulī ā nūllō crēditur.
The consul is trusted by nobody.

| Practice sentences on the impersonal use of verbs in the passive.

Translate into English or Latin as appropriate.

1. **quattuor hōrās pugnātum est, sed tum hostēs nostrīs nōn iam restitērunt.**
2. **prīncipī ab omnibus pārēbātur sed is sōlum paucīs fauēbat.**
3. **postquam in campum uentum est, urbī appropinquāuimus.**
4. I obey the general but I do not trust him. (*Use the impersonal construction.*)
5. The battle was long and fierce. (*Use the impersonal construction.*)

Gerunds and gerundives

By <u>walking</u> more quickly, he made faster progress.
She prefers <u>walking</u> to <u>running</u>.
He is addicted to <u>eating</u> sweets.

In these sentences the words *walking*, *running*, and *eating* are gerunds.
Gerunds are verbal nouns, i.e. nouns formed from verbs. In English they
end in *-ing*, and can easily be confused with participles (see above, pp.
76–7). Thus, while in the second sentence above *walking* and *running* are
gerunds, in the sentence *The walking man beat the running boy* the words
are adjectives. If in doubt, put the words 'the act (*or* action) of' in front of
the word ending in *-ing*. They will always make some sort or sense in front
of a gerund but will be meaningless before a participle.

Note that in English the gerund can take an object, e.g. *eating sweets* in
the third sentence above.

The gerund and gerundive in Latin

In Latin the present infinitive active supplies the nominative and accusative
of the gerund. In the other cases **-andī** or **-andō** is added to the stem of first
conjugation verbs, and **-endī** or **-endō** to the stem of all other verbs, including deponents. After prepositions governing the accusative, a gerund ending
in **-andum** or **-endum** is used, and not the infinitive. **The gerund is neuter.**

Nom.	parāre (*to prepare,* *preparing*)	monēre (*to advise,* *advising*)	regere (*to rule,* *ruling*)	audīre (*to hear,* *hearing*)
Gen.	parandī	monendī	regendī	audiendī
Dat.	parandō	monendō	regendō	audiendō
Acc.	parāre, parandum	monēre, monendum	regere, regendum	audīre, audiendum
Abl.	parandō	monendō	regendō	audiendō

amāre dulce est
Loving is delightful.

ars amandī
the art of loving

studuit amandō
He devoted himself to loving.

nescit amāre
He does not know how to love. (*Literally*, he does not know loving.)

parātus ad amandum
ready for loving

fēminās amandō
by loving women

The last example above is not, in fact, ideal Latin. While the gerund can take an object in English, Latin usually prefers to harmonize the endings of the gerund and its object. (The process is known as 'gerundival attraction', a faintly comic expression which makes it sound more difficult than it is.)

fēminās amandō   by loving women

Clearly the ablative must not be changed; if it is, the meaning by will be lost. The object of the gerund must therefore be put into the case of the gerund, which then becomes an adjective (ending in *-andus, -a, -um* or *-endus, -a, -um*) which then agrees with the noun. This adjective is called the 'gerundive'. Thus we have **fēminīs amandīs.**

ars cīuēs regendī 'the art of ruling the citizens' becomes **ars cīuium regendōrum**.

☑ Note:

1. Gerundival attraction always occurs (a) after prepositions; (b) when the gerund is in the dative.
2. Gerundival attraction tends to be avoided (a) with neuter pronouns or adjectives in the genitive, dative, or ablative; (b) when the meaning of the verb is stressed; (c) by some authors when it would lead to a repetition of first and second declension endings in the genitive plural. Thus **ars librōs legendī** may be preferable to the cumbrous **ars librōrum legendōrum**.

····➤ **Note**

1 ad + the gerund or gerundive (by attraction) expressing purpose, e.g.

ad pācem petendam   for the purpose of seeking peace.

2 The postpositions (prepositions placed after the nouns they govern) **causā** and **grātiā** (both with the genitive) 'for the sake of':

pācis petendae causā (or **grātiā**)

for the sake of seeking peace, *i.e.* in order to seek peace.

3 Nouns which take a 'determining' genitive (see examples), such as **occāsiō, occāsiōnis**, *f.* (opportunity), **facultās, facultātis**, *f.* (opportunity), **signum, signī**, n. (sign, signal), and adjectives which govern a noun in the genitive, such as **cupidus, -a, -um** (eager) and **perītus, -a, -um** (skilled), are followed, reasonably enough, by the genitive of the gerund or gerundive:

occāsiō amandī

an opportunity for loving, *i.e.* a chance to love

signum oppugnandī

the signal to attack

signum oppidī oppugnandī

the signal to attack the town (gerundive)

cupidus edendī

eager to eat (*literally*, desirous of eating)

perītus docendī

experienced in teaching

4 The following usages with verbs of entrusting and undertaking, e.g. **dō, dare, dedī, datum** (I give), **cūrō** (1) (I see to) and **suscipiō, suscipere, suscēpī, susceptum** (I undertake):

librum legendum puellae dedī.

I gave the girl a book to read.

pontem aedificandum cūrāuit.

He saw to the building of the bridge.

suscēpit nāuēs reficiendās.

He undertook the repair of the ships.

5 The gerund of **eō** (I go) is **eundum**. The form **faciundum** (instead of **faciendum** (from **faciō** I make, do) is common in old Latin. Note also the expression (**pecūniae**) **repetundae**, *f.pl.*, meaning *extortion of money*.

Practice sentences on the gerund and gerundive can be found at the foot of the following section (the Gerundive of Obligation).

| The gerundive of obligation

This film is on no account <u>to be missed</u>.
One thing remains <u>to be done</u>.

The gerundive in Latin is a passive verbal adjective (the equivalent of *to be missed*, *to be done* in the above sentences). Its endings are the same as that of the gerund save that it is an adjective ending in **-us, -a, -um** (e.g. **monendus, -a, -um**). When combined with the verb **esse** (to be) it expresses ideas of obligation (e.g. 'ought', 'must', 'should' 'have to'), and is therefore called 'the gerundive of obligation'.

| 1. The gerundive with transitive verbs

librum legō.
I read the book.

liber legitur.
The book is read.

liber legendus est.
The book is to-be-read, *i.e.* The book must be (should be, ought to be, has to be) read.

liber legendus erat.
The book was to-be-read, *i.e.* The book had to be read.

When negatived the gerundive can express ideas of permissibility or appropriateness, e.g.

rēs nōn contemnenda   a thing not to be despised.

Remember that the gerundive is passive in meaning.

The agent goes into the dative.

liber mihi legendus est.
The book is to-be-read by me, *i.e.* I must read the book.

puella tibi amanda est.
You must love the girl.

urbs nōbīs relinquenda est.
We must leave the city.

Note:
This pattern is followed only with transitive verbs which have their objects in the accusative.

| 2. The gerundive with intransitive verbs

The gerundive of intransitive verbs and verbs followed by cases other than the accusative (see list on p. 11) must be used *impersonally* (i.e. when translating into English, start with the word 'it', but remember that you may have to adjust your literal translation to achieve a stylish result) (see pp. 104–5).

ab urbe nōbīs discēdendum est.
It is to-be-left from the city by us, *i.e.* We must leave the city.[1]····>

prīmā lūce nōbīs prōgrediendum est.
We must set out at dawn.

mihi errantī ignōscendum est.
I must be forgiven when I make a mistake.

lēgibus pārendum est.
The laws must be obeyed.

····> 1. *Compare* urbs nōbīs relinquenda est.

 Note:
As we have seen, the agent normally goes into the dative. However, if a dative of the agent was inserted in the last sentence above, where the object of the verb (**lēgibus**) is in the dative, an ambiguity would arise: **lēgibus nōbīs pārendum est** could mean *either* 'We must obey the laws' *or* 'The laws must obey us'. In such cases **ā** or **ab** with the ablative is used with the agent, i.e. **lēgibus ā nōbīs pārendum est**.

| Practice sentences on gerunds and gerundives

Translate into English or Latin as appropriate:

1. omnia ūnō tempore erant agenda.
2. agrōs Heluetiīs habitandōs dedit.
3. hostibus ā nōbīs parcendum est.
4. Titus equitandī perītissimus fuit.
5. sapientia ars uīuendī putanda est. (Cicero, de finibus, 1.42)
6. ūnus homō nōbīs cunctandō restituit rem. (Ennius, quoted in Cicero, de officiis, 1.84)
7. I must cross the sea. (*Use gerundive.*)
8. Always eager to read, he was a glutton (helluo, (gen.) helluonis, *m.* + gen.) for books.
9. & I am sending scouts to find the legate.
10. (*Two ways, both involving the gerund.*)
11. Soldiers must obey generals.
12. By reading books, he becomes wiser every day.

Conditional sentences

Conditional clauses are introduced by *if, unless, if . . . not, whether . . . or.*
Conditional sentences are made up of a conditional clause and a main clause
giving the result or inference of the conditional clause. In both English and
Latin the conditional clause usually (but by no means always) comes first.

If there are puddles in the road this morning, it rained last night.
If it rains later today, there will be puddles in the road.
If it were to rain, there would be puddles in the road.
If it had rained, there would have been puddles in the road.

In both English and Latin, conditional sentences can simply state facts, as in
the first two sentences above and in the axiomatic

If a triangle has two equal sides, it is an isosceles triangle.

In this grammar we call these conditionals 'open' and the verbs in both the
'if' clause (the **protasis**) and the main clause (the **apodosis**) are–quite naturally, since they state facts–in the tense of the *indicative* which suits their
sense.

The third and fourth sentences above fall into the category of the 'remote'
and the 'unfulfilled' respectively. Comparison between the second and third
sentences will show how the third is expressed in a doubtful or remote way
in contrast with the second. The words 'were to' and 'would' (English
equivalents of the subjunctive) signal this remoteness.

In the fourth sentence, we are in the area of the unreal or the impossible.
It did not rain and so the condition is unfulfilled. Here the words 'would
have' are the key. The subjunctive in Latin conditionals will lead inevitably
to the use of the word 'would' in the main clause of an English translation.
In Latin the verbs in both halves in 'remote' or 'unfulfilled' conditionals are
in the subjunctive.

 Note:
The Latin for 'if' is **sī**, for 'if not' or 'unless' **nisi** (but see point 4 on
pp. 116–17).

| Open conditions

The appropriate tenses of the indicative are used in Latin:

sī hoc dīxit, errāuit.
If he said that, he was wrong.

sī dīligenter labōrātis, discipulī meī, ualdē gaudeō.
If you are working hard, my students, I am very happy.

sī mē uīsere uīs, Rōmam uenī.
If you want to see me, come to Rome.

sī domum meam uēneris/ueniēs, libenter tē salūtābō.
If you come to my house, I shall welcome you warmly.

In the last sentence a problem arises because of the difference between Latin and English. English tends to use a 'concealed future' (that is to say, 'you come' looks like a present tense, but in fact means 'you will come' or 'you will have come'). Latin here *must* use the future or, if the action will be complete before the result, the future perfect. When translating from English into Latin, watch out for these concealed futures in the English.

| Remote and unfulfilled conditions

These are always identifiable in English by the use of the word 'would' in the main clause (*apodosis*). In Latin the *subjunctive* is used in both clauses. The present subjunctive refers to future time–there is no future subjunctive–, the imperfect subjunctive refers to present time, and the pluperfect subjunctive to past time.

Future	**present subjunctive**	**sī dīligenter labōrēs, prōficiās.**
		If you worked (were to work) hard, you would make progress.
Present	**imperfect subjunctive**	**sī dīligenter labōrārēs, prōficerēs.**
		If you were working hard, you would be making progress.
Past	**pluperfect subjunctive**	**sī dīligenter labōrāuissēs, prōfēcissēs.**
		If you had worked hard, you would have made progress.

☑ **Note:**
Like English, Latin can make a distinction between past and present
time between the clauses, e.g.

sī dīligenter labōrāuissēs, iam prōficerēs.
If you had worked hard, you would now be making progress.

····▶ **Note**

1 The English 'subjunctive' words 'were to', 'would', 'would have'.

2 If the verb in the Latin main clause (**apodosis**) of a past unfulfilled conditional sentence means 'can', 'must', 'is proper, necessary', e.g. **possum** (I can), **dēbeō** (I
ought), **oportet** (it is necessary or proper, 'should'), or **sum** (I am) with a gerundive
of obligation (see pp. 111–12), it is regularly in the indicative (imperfect or perfect,
rarely pluperfect). These verbs contain within themselves a subjunctive type of
meaning (e.g. 'could', 'should'):

   sī hoc fēcissēs, pūniendus fuistī (or **erās**).
   If you had done this, you should have been punished.

3 The 'double conditional' words, **seu . . . seu . . .** (before consonants) *or*
sīue . . . sīue . . . (whether . . . or . . .):

   seu mē rūrī uīseris seu Rōmae mānseris, contentus erō.
   Whether you come to see me in the country or stay in Rome, I shall be
   content.

   sīue minus is used for 'if not' without a verb:
   sīue mē uīseris sīue minus . . .
   Whether you come to see me or not . . .

   Note that **sī minus** (if not) can also be used without a verb.

4 **nisi** = unless, if not:
   nisi mē uīseris, trīstissimus manēbō.
   Unless you come to see me, I shall remain very sad.

   sī nōn = if not *is used*:
   (a) when the main clause (**apodosis**) contains **at**, **tamen**, or **certē** (yet, still, even
   so, at least, none the less, certainly):
   sī mihi bonā rē pūblicā fruī nōn licuerit, at carēbō malā. [(Cicero, pro
   Milone, 93)]
   If I am not allowed to enjoy good government, I shall at least be free of bad.

(b) when the same verb is repeated:

hoc sī fēceris, habēbō grātiam; sī nōn fēceris, ignōscam.
If you have done this, I shall be grateful; if you haven't done it, I shall forgive you.

(c) when individual words are contrasted:

cum spē, sī nōn optimā, at aliquā tamen uīuit.
He lives with some hopes, if not the highest.

5 **quodsī** and **sīn** both mean *but if*.

6 **sī quis** = *if anyone* **nisi quis** = *unless anyone* **sī quandō** = *if ever*

7 As in English the 'if' clause can come first or second in Latin:

habēbō grātiam sī hoc fēceris.
I shall be grateful if you do this.

| Practice sentences

Translate into English or Latin as appropriate:

1. **respīrābō sī tē uīderō**. (Cicero, ad Atticum, 2.24.5)
2. **respīrem sī tē uideam**.
3. **nēmō ferē saltat sōbrius nisi forte īnsānit**. (Cicero, pro Murena, 13)
4. **nisi ante Rōmā prōfectus essēs, nunc eam certē relinquerēs**. (Cicero, ad familiares, 7.11.1)
5. **nōn possem uīuere nisi in litterīs uīuerem**.
6. **hunc hominem, sī ūlla in tē esset pietās, colere dēbēbās**.
7. If you come to Italy, I beg you to visit me at Rome.
8. If you were to come to Rhodes, I would show you the Colossus.
9. If she has done what (id quod) I asked, I shall thank her.
10. If Cicero had fled the country, he would not have been killed.
11. If you were helping me, I would be much happier.
12. What would you say if I spat (spuo, spuere) in your face?
13. Whether you like my poems or hate them, I hope you will come to my recital.
14. If you had learnt my poems, you could have recited them to your sister.

Time clauses

The beggar left the city <u>before the senate house burnt down</u>.
The mouse hurried off <u>before the cat spotted it</u>.
The mouse hurried off <u>before the cat could spot it</u>.

In the first of the sentences above, the time clause simply tells us when the beggar left the city: there is presumably no connection between his departure and the fire. In the second sentence there is probably an implication of purpose: the mouse hurried off in order to avoid being spotted by the cat. In the third sentence, the suggestion of purpose is made explicit by the use of the English 'subjunctive' *could*.

Latin uses the indicative in time clauses of the first kind (the vast majority) and the subjunctive in time clauses of the third kind. What difference would the use of (a) an indicative and (b) a subjunctive make in a Latin version of the second sentence above? Compare this pair of Latin sentences:

> **priusquam Caesar peruēnit, obsidēs poposcit.**
> Before Caesar arrived, he demanded hostages.

> **collem celeriter priusquam ab hostibus cōnspicerētur commūnīuit.**
> He quickly fortified the hill before he was (could be) noticed by the enemy.

The following words introduce time clauses:

cum[1]····➤ **ubi**[2]····➤ } **ut**	when
cum/ubi/ut prīmum } **simul atque/ac**	as soon as
antequam } **priusquam**	before
postquam } **posteāquam**	after

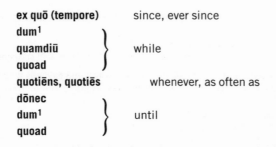

ex quō (tempore)	since, ever since
dum[1]	
quamdiū	while
quoad	
quotiēns, quotiēs	whenever, as often as
dōnec	
dum[1]	until
quoad	

····➤ 1. **cum** and **dum** are used differently from other 'time' conjunctions. See separate entries on pp. 122–5.

····➤ 2. Note that **ubi** is used meaning 'when' in time clauses; **quandō?** is used meaning 'when?' in direct and indirect questions. Remember that **ubi** also means 'where'.

As we have said, the words which introduce time clauses are regularly followed by the indicative in the tense that the meaning requires.

····➤ Note

1 The 'concealed future'.

nōn tē uidēbō antequam Rōmam uēneris.
I shall not see you before you come (will have come) to Rome.

Here Latin uses the future perfect (*not* the future), whereas English uses the present tense relating to the future. **nōn . . . antequam** is the equivalent of **postquam** and the action of the time clause must happen and *be complete* before the action of the main clause.

BUT **antequam** can be followed by a present indicative when the main verb is not negative:

antequam ad sententiam redeō, dē mē pauca dīcam. (Cicero, in Catilinam, 4.20)
Before I return to the subject, I shall say a few things about myself.

2 **postquam (posteāquam)**, **ubi**, **ut**, **simul atque (simul ac)**, **ut prīmum**, and **cum prīmum** are all followed by the perfect indicative when they refer to past time:

Pompēius ut equitātum suum pulsum uīdit, aciē excessit.

(Caesar, de bello civili, 3.94.5)
When Pompey saw his cavalry beaten, he left the battle line.

English is likely to say When 'Pompey *had* seen . . .' while Latin uses the perfect.

BUT in Latin the pluperfect is used with **post** . . . **quam** when a definite interval of time is mentioned:

post diem tertium gesta rēs est quam dīxerat. (Cicero, pro Milone, 44)
The matter was dealt with on the third day (i.e. two days) after he had spoken.

3 The pluperfect is also used after **ubi, ut, simul atque (simul ac)**, and **quotiēns** when the action of the verb has occurred repeatedly in the past (as after 'whenever' in English).

ubi litterās tuās accēperam, ualdē gaudēbam.
Whenever I received a letter from you, I was very happy.

The perfect is also used frequently in this sense in primary sequence:

ubi litterās tuās accēpī, ualdē gaudeō.
Whenever I receive a letter from you, I am very happy.

When the repeated action refers to the present or the future, *quotiēns* is used followed by the appropriate tense of the indicative.

4 The words **antequam, postquam**, and **posteāquam** are often split in two, the first bit going in the main clause, as in the second example in **2** above. There is no problem in translating into English if you hold up the translation of the words **ante, post** or **posteā** until you reach the word **quam** and translate it there.

ante ad urbem celeriter rediī quam tu Capuam aduēnistī.
I returned quickly to the city before you came to Capua.

5 Remember that if there is any idea of *purpose, expectation* or *waiting for something to happen*, the verb in the time clause goes into the subjunctive:

mūs celeriter effūgit priusquam fēlēs salīret.
The mouse hurried off before the cat could leap.

6 The verb in a time clause naturally goes into the subjunctive when this is a subordinate clause in indirect statement.

| Practice sentences

Translate into English or Latin as appropriate:

1. **simul atque hoc fēcī, scīuī mē errāuisse.**
2. **Hamilcar nōnō annō postquam in Hispāniam uēnerat, occīsus est.** (Nepos, 22.4.2)
3. **nōn prius respondēbō quam tacueris.**
4. **ubi rēgīna hoc fēcerat, rēx ualdē īrātus fīēbat.**
5. **ē iānuā effūgī priusquam coniūnx mea mē uituperāret.**

6. She left the city before I saw her.
7. She left the city before I could see her.
8. Don't do this before the king arrives.
9. Whenever she does that, I love her even more.
10. I killed her before she could kill me.

Cum (= when)

cum illud fēceris, īrātus erō.
When you do that, I shall be angry.

cum illud fēcissēs, īrātus fuī.
When you did that, I was angry.

When the verb in the *cum* clause is in a primary tense (see pp. 86–7), it is in the indicative. (Watch out for the 'concealed future or future perfect' as in the first example above.) When the verb in the **cum** clause is in a historic tense, it is in the subjunctive. This will always be *either* an imperfect subjunctive *or* a pluperfect subjunctive according to the sense (<u>never perfect</u>).

However, if there is a temporal adverb (e.g. **tum, tunc** (then), **nunc, iam** (now)) or a temporal expression (e.g. involving the words **tempus** (time) or **diēs** (day)) in the main clause, a historic tense of the indicative can be found in the time clause. In such sentences, the idea will be purely to do with time (i.e. there will be no hint of cause and effect between the time clause and the main clause):

sex librōs dē rēpūblicā tum scrīpsī cum gubernācula reī pūblicae tenēbam.
(Cicero, de diuinatione, 2.3)
I wrote six books about the state in the period when I was holding the reins of power.

☑ Note:

If it is the main clause and not the apparent time clause which contains the idea of time, the indicative is always used after **cum**:
sōl occidēbat cum aduēnī.
The sun was setting when I arrived.

This is known as 'inverted **cum**'. Here the *cum* clause will naturally come second.

'Inverted **cum**' can also be used when the *cum* clause contains the more important contents. It often communicates a surprise, e.g.:

Hannibal iam subībat mūrōs cum repente ērumpunt Rōmānī. (Livy, 29.7.8)
Hannibal was already approaching the walls when suddenly the Romans
burst out.

Some further uses of <u>Cum</u>

1. **cum** = <u>whenever</u>, <u>as often as</u>

   cum eum uīderō   (future time–future perfect indicative)
   whenever I see him

   cum eum uīdī   (present time–perfect indicative)
   whenever I see him

   cum eum uīderam   (past time–pluperfect indicative)
   whenever I saw him

2. **cum** = <u>since</u>

   quae cum ita sint
   since these things are so

   quae cum ita essent
   since these things were so

cum meaning 'since' is always followed by the subjunctive, in the tense
which best suits the meaning.

3. **cum** = <u>although</u>, <u>whereas</u>

   **cum prīmī ordinēs hostium concidissent, tamen acerrimē relīquī
   resistēbant.** (Caesar, de bello Gallico, 7.62.4)
   Although the first ranks of the enemy had fallen, the rest still (none the
   less, nevertheless) resisted most vigorously.

cum meaning 'although' is always followed by the subjunctive.

 Note:

To make it clear that **cum** means 'although', **tamen** is often included in
the main clause (as in the sentence above).

Practice sentences on **'cum'** *are included in the exercise at the foot of the*
*following chapter (***Dum** = *while).*

Dum (= while)

> I nodded off from time to time while the instructor was talking.
> While the pile-driver was running, I could not hear a word you were saying.

In English the word 'while' tends to be used either with the meaning 'in the course of the time that . . .', as in the first sentence above, or, less frequently, to mean 'exactly as long as . . .', 'all the time that . . .', as in the second sentence.

For the former, far more common, meaning, Latin rather remarkably uses the present indicative in the 'while' clause, even in an indirect statement. But when 'while' means 'exactly as long as . . .', the verb goes into the natural tense of the indicative–which will regularly be the same as that of the main verb. So:

dum fēlēs abest, mūrēs lūdent

means something different from

dum fēlēs aberit, mūrēs lūdent.

The first sentence means that the mice will indulge in more or less play while the cat is away, the second that they will play every moment of its absence.

Think about the difference in meaning between:

dum haec geruntur, ego rīdēbam.
dum haec gerēbantur, ego rīdēbam.

Some further uses of Dum

1. **dum** = until: the same rules apply as with other regular time words (see pp. 118–20):

    manē hīc dum sōl occiderit.
    Stay here until after sunset (*Literally*, until the sun shall have set).

exspectā dum litterās meās accipiās.
Wait until you get my letter (*the idea of purpose*).

2. **dum, dummodo** = provided that, if only, as long as:

ōderint dum metuant. (Accius, Atreus, fragment 4)
Let them hate provided that they fear.

dum hoc nē agās, tūtus eris.
As long as you don t do this, you will be safe.

In these clauses, Latin regularly uses the subjunctive, negative **nē**.

3. **dum** = while, in a causal sense, i.e. because, in that:

dum ōtium uolunt etiam sine dignitāte retinēre, ipsī utrumque āmittunt.
(Cicero, pro Sestio, 100)
While (because, in that) they wish to keep their leisure even at the price
of their dignity, they themselves lose them both.

Here Latin uses the indicative.

| Practice sentences on 'cum' and 'dum'

Translate into English or Latin as appropriate:

1. **Zēnōnem cum Athēnīs essem audiēbam frequenter.** (Cicero, de natura deorum, 1.21.59)
2. **dum haec Rōmae aguntur, cōnsulēs ambō in Liguribus gerēbant bellum.** (Livy, 39.1.1)
3. **cum rosam uīderat, tum incipere uēr arbitrābātur.** (Cicero, in Verrem, 2.5.27)
4. **Tiberius Gracchus tam diū laudābitur dum memoria rērum Rōmānārum manēbit.** (Cicero, de officiis, 2.43)
5. **dolō erat pugnandum, cum pār nōn esset armīs.** (Nepos, 23.10.4)
6. Although (*use* cum) they hate the emperor, they still obey him.
7. While Horatius was reciting his poetry, people sometimes (aliquando) laughed.
8. When you see my sister, greet her warmly (comiter).
9. He stayed in Rome until he could see the consul.
10. Since you are my enemy I shall not trust you.

Because, although, as if

Because

> Socrates was executed because he had corrupted young men.
> Socrates was executed on the grounds that he had corrupted young men.

The first of these English sentences gives the actual reason for the execution of Socrates. The second gives an alleged reason, possibly an untrue one.

In Latin the difference is indicated by the use of **quod**, **quia**, or **quoniam** followed by the indicative when the actual reason is given, and by the use of **quod** followed by the subjunctive when an alleged reason is given. (An alleged reason is a thought in someone's head and is thus in effect a subordinate clause in indirect statement.)

What is the difference in meaning between these two sentences?

> **puella culpāta est quod librum incenderat.**
> **puella culpāta est quod librum incendisset.**

quod followed by the indicative or the subjunctive (depending on the distinction given above) is frequently used after verbs of emotion, e.g.

aegrē ferō	I am sorry that . . .
doleō (2)	I am sorry
gaudeō (2)	I am glad
laetor (1)	I am glad
mīror (1)	I wonder

> **uehementer laetor quod scrīpsistī.**
> I am extremely glad that you have written.

But all of these verbs are more commonly followed by the accusative + infinitive or by *sī* (if) than by a *quod* clause.

••••▶ Note

1 **nōn quod** or **nōn quō** (not because) introduces a rejected reason and the verb in such a clause, like that in an alleged reason, goes into the subjunctive. If the actual reason follows, it is introduced by **sed quia** and its verb is in the indicative.

in uīllā mānsit, nōn quod aeger esset, sed quia ego aderam.
He stayed in the villa not because he was sick but because I was there.

2 The reason can be emphasized by including **eō, idcircō, ideō**, or **proptereā** (all meaning 'for this reason') in the main clause.

Quīntum idcircō uītāuī quod eum ōderam.
I avoided Quintus precisely because I hated him.

3 For **cum** meaning 'because' or 'since', see p. 123.

| Although

Although you did no work, you still passed the exam.
Even if you did no work, you would still pass the exam.

Clauses beginning with the words 'although', 'though', 'even though', or 'even if' are known as concessive clauses. They can deal *either* with facts, as in the first sentence above (in which it is taken as true that 'you did no work'), *or* with possibilities, as in the second sentence (in which you may or may not do some work).

In Latin the factual concessive clauses are introduced by **quamquam, etsī**, or **tametsī** (or **sī** in Latin poetry), **etiam sī**, or **etiamsī**, and their verb is in the indicative:

quamquam dīligenter labōrāuistī, tamen errāuistī.
Although you worked hard, you still made a mistake.

The concessive clauses dealing with possibilities are introduced by **quamuīs, etsī. etiam sī**, or **etiamsī**, and the verb goes into the subjunctive.

quamuīs dīligenter labōrēs, tamen errās.
However hard you may be working, you are still wrong.

(Notice the use of **tamen** in the main clause to reinforce the meaning 'although'.)

etsī, etiam sī, and **etiamsī** are compounds of **sī** and mean 'even *if*'. Therefore, when they are followed by a subjunctive, the tense of that subjunctive will be the one called for in a conditional clause (see p. 115).

····▶ Note
1 **quamuīs** = 'however' with an adjective or adverb. When used in this way, it is always followed by the subjunctive.

quamuīs dīligenter labōrēs, nōn prōficiēs.
However hard you work, you will not succeed.
(The literal meaning of the **quamuīs** clause is something like 'You may work hard as much as you wish'.)

2   **quamuīs** = 'however' can be used as an adverb with an adjective or adverb:

quamuīs fortis, tamen effūgit.
However brave (he was), he still ran away.

3   **licet** + subjunctive = even though:

licet undique perīcula impendeant, tamen ea subībō.
Although dangers threaten me on every side, I shall still face them.
(The literal meaning of the *licet* clause is something like 'Let dangers threaten me on every side–it is permitted [to them to do so]'.)

4   For **cum** = 'although', see p. 123.

| As if, as (comparisons)

The senators were terribly afraid, as if the enemy were already at the gates of Rome.
The general was rewarded as his courage deserved.

In the first of these sentences, the comparison is untrue. The enemy were not at the gates of Rome. In the second sentence, the comparison is true. The general's courage did deserve to be rewarded.

In Latin if the verb conveys a fact (as in the second meaning above), it is naturally in the indicative since it is true. If the verb makes an imaginary (i.e. untrue) comparison (as with the first meaning above), it is in the subjunctive. Comparisons are much more likely to be untrue than true.

Among the Latin words and expressions for 'as if' or 'as though' are:

perinde ac (sī)	**tamquam sī**
quasi	**uelut**
sīcut	**uelut sī**
tamquam	**ut (sī)**

ut merita est, poenās persoluit.
She was punished as she deserved.
tamquam merita esset, poenōs persoluit.
She was punished as if she had deserved it.

····➤ Note

1 The tense of the subjunctive is usually determined by the sequence of tenses (see pp. 86–7), *not* the rules for conditional sentences.

2 **haud aliter ac/atque** = not otherwise than:

haud aliter locūtus est ac solēbat.
He spoke as he always did (*literally*, not otherwise than he was accustomed to).

| Practice sentences

Translate into English or Latin as appropriate:

1. **Rōmānī quamquam itinere fessī erant, tamen obuiam hostibus prōcessērunt.**
2. **Aristīdēs nōnne ob eam causam expulsus est patriā quod praeter modum iūstus esset?** (Cicero, Tusculan Disputations, 5.105)
3. **quamuīs sīs molestus, numquam tē esse cōnfitēbor malum.** (Cicero, Tusculan Disputations, 2.62)
4. **hīc est obstandum, mīlitēs, uelut sī ante Rōmāna moenia pugnēmus.** (Livy, 21.41.15)
5. **Quīntum paenitet quod animum tuum offendit.**
6. **tanta est tempestās quantam numquam anteā uīdī.**
7. I was extremely happy that my husband had died.
8. Although I was walking fast, I could not avoid the bore (molestus ille).
9. However fast you walk, you will not escape me.
10. He was praised because he had saved the state; but in fact (re uera) Cicero did that.
11. He was praised not because he had saved the state but because he wrote good poems.
12. He looked (i.e. appeared) as if he was sick, but in fact he was angry.

Quīn and quōminus

Quīn

> I do not doubt that she is a respectable woman.
> Nothing will prevent me from coming to your birthday party.

The English verbs 'doubt', 'deny', 'hinder', and 'prevent' are followed by a number of different expressions. Latin often uses **quīn** followed by the subjunctive (the tense depending on the sequence of tenses, see pp. 86–7) after a **negative** main verb with one of these meanings (e.g. **nōn dubitō** (1) 'I do not doubt', **nōn negō** (1) 'I do not deny', **nōn impediō** (4) 'I do not hinder, prevent'). The Latin for the sentences above could be:

> **nōn dubitō quīn pudīca sit.**
> **nihil mē impediet quīn nātālī tuō adsim.**

The word **quīn** causes English speakers problems because it does not translate into idiomatic English. Literally, it means 'by which not'. The old-fashioned 'but that' may be useful as a first stage in translation:

> I do not doubt <u>but that</u> she is a respectable woman.

> **nōn dubitāuit quīn Germānī oppugnātūrī essent.**
> He did not doubt that the Germans were going to attack.

> **nōn negāuit quīn ipse scelus admīsisset.**
> He did not deny that he himself had committed the crime.

> **nōn tē impediam quīn proficīscāris.**
> I shall not prevent you from setting out.

As we have seen, the main verb before **quīn** will be negative. Sometimes the words **uix** or **aegrē** (scarcely) are found instead of a plain negative (they are known as 'virtual negatives'). A question expecting the answer 'no' (**num . . .?**) or implying the answer 'no' (who doubts that . . .? *can imply* no one doubts that . . .) may also come before **quīn**.

> **uix quisquam dubitāre potest quīn stultus sīs.**
> Scarcely anyone can doubt that you are a fool.

> **num quisquam dubitāre potuit quīn sapiēns essēs?**
> Surely no one could have doubted that you were wise.

Note the following common expressions:
- **haud (nōn) dubium est quīn . . .**
  there is no doubt that . . .
- **haud dubitārī potest quīn . . .**
  it cannot be doubted that . . .
- **haud multum (or minimum) āfuit quīn . . .**
  almost (*literally*, it was not much (*or* very little) distant but that . . .)
    > **haud multum āfuit quīn interficerer.** (impersonal)
    > I was almost killed.

or

> **haud multum āfuī quīn interficerer.**
> *Literally*, I was not much distant . . . (personal).

- **nōn possum facere quīn . . .**
  I cannot help . . .
- **nōn potest fierī quīn . . .**
  it is impossible that . . . not
- **nēmō est quīn . . .**
  there is nobody who . . . not
    > **nēmō est quīn hoc sciat.**
    > Everybody knows this.

| Quōminus

quōminus is used with much the same meaning as **quīn** ('but that' in old-fashioned English) after verbs of *hindering* and *preventing* **whether negatived or not**. As with **quīn**, the main problem here for English-speakers is that **quōminus**, which literally means 'by which the less', does not translate into idiomatic English.

> **(nōn) mē impedīuit quōminus in urbem inīrem.**
> He prevented (didn't prevent) me from going into the city.

Note the following common idioms:
- **per mē stat quōminus . . .**
  it is due to me that . . . not
  per mē stetit quōminus rēs pūblica ēuerterētur.
  It was due to me that the republic was not overthrown.

- **per me stetit** *ut . . .*
  it was due to me that . . .

  per mē stetit ut rēs pūblica cōnseruārētur.
  It was due to me that the republic was saved.

Note that **prohibeō** (2) (I prevent) can be followed simply by the infinitive.

prohibuī eum Rōmā ēgredī.
I prevented him from leaving Rome.

It can also be followed by **nē** or **quōminus** or, when negative, **quīn**, all with the subjunctive.

| Practice sentences

Translate into English or Latin as appropriate:

1. **nōn dubitārī dēbet quīn fuerint ante Homērum poētae.** (Cicero, *Brutus*, 71)
2. **nōn dēterret sapientem mors quōminus in omne tempus reī pūblicae cōnsulat.** (Cicero, *Tusculan Disputations*, 1.91)
3. **facere nōn possum quīn litterās cottīdiē ad tē mittam.** (Cicero, *ad Atticum*, 12.27.2)
4. **nihil abest quīn sim miserrimus.** (Cicero, *ad Atticum*, 11.15.3)
5. **impedīuit eam coniūnx quōminus amātōrem uīseret.**
6. I almost died laughing (use quin—for 'laughing' use the ablative of the gerund).
7. Who can prevent me from leaving Rome?
8. I could not help admiring your poems.
9. It is due to me that you are so rich.
10. Everyone knows that Homer was the greatest of poets (*use* quin).

Some, any, every, each, ever

Some

1. **aliquis**   someone—it could be anyone
   - Also used to mean 'a somebody' in the sense of a person of consequence.

   aliquid   something–it could be anything

   aliquī, aliqua, aliquod   some . . . it could be any (adjectival)

   quīdam, quaedam, quoddam   some–not any but a particular . . .
   - Literally a certain–it usually follows its noun

     fēmina quaedam   a certain woman, some woman, a woman
   - There is no word for 'a' or 'an' in Latin: **quīdam** and **aliquis** are the closest equivalents.

   nescioquis, nescioquid   someone, something
   - Literally, I do not know who or what—cf. French **je ne sais quoi**–something or other

   nōnnūllī   some (of number)

   aliquot (indeclinable adjective)   some (of number)

   complūrēs   some, several

2. **ali-** in front of 'question words' (see p. 92) gives those words the meaning 'some':

   aliquantum (with partitive genitive)   some amount of

   alicubi   somewhere

   aliquamdiū   for some while

   aliquandō   at some time, sometimes, now and then

3. **aliī . . . aliī . . .**   some . . . others . . .

If the word **alius** is repeated in a different case, the meaning is doubled, as here:

> **aliī alia dīcunt.**
> Some people say some things, others (say) other things.

The two **alius** words must come next or very close to each other to convey this double meaning.

Any

quisquam	anyone (with prohibitions, negatives, virtual negatives (**uix** and **aegrē**), with questions expecting the answer no (**num...?**) and after **quam** (= than))

● Latin uses **nec quisquam** and not **et nēmō**.

ūllus	any (adjective corresponding to **quisquam** though stronger in meaning)
quīuīs, quaeuīs, quoduīs (adjective) *or* **quiduīs** (pronoun)	any(body) (you like), any(thing) (you like)
quīlibet, quaelibet, quodlibet (adjective) *or* **quidlibet** (pronoun)	any(body) (you like), any(thing) (you like)
quis, quid	anyone (after **sī**, **nisi**, **num**, **nē**, **quō**, **quantō**)
quī, qua *or* **quae, quod**	any . . . (adjective of **quis**)

Every, each

1.	**quisque, quaeque quidque**	every one, each one each one, each thing

Note:

quisque is used especially with superlatives, ordinal numbers, and with **sē** and **suus**, e.g.:

sapientissimus quisque
All the wisest men

septimus quisque
Every seventh man

sē quisque adiuuet
Let each man help himself.

---

uterque   each of two
uterque fīlius
each son of two, i.e. both sons

 Note:

Though two sons are referred to, the singular is used here, because **uterque** means 'each <u>one</u> of two'.

---

2. **-que** added to question words (see p. 92) gives these words the meaning 'every':

ubīque   everywhere
undique   from everywhere
but
utrimque   from both sides

Ever

1 **-cumque** added to relatives = ever

quīcumque, quaecumque, quodcumque	whoever, whatever
quāliscumque	of whatever sort
ubicumque	wherever
quōcumque	to wherever
quotiēnscumque	whenever, however often

2. Note:

quisquis	whoever	(both are used only in the nominative and ablative singular)
quidquid	whatever	
quotquot	however many	(indeclinable adjective)
quōquō	to wherever	
sīcubi	if anywhere	
nēcubi	lest anywhere	

| Practice sentences

Translate into English or Latin as appropriate:

1. **disertōs cognōuī nōnnūllōs, ēloquentem nēminem.**
2. **quīdam dē plēbē prōdiit ad ōrātiōnem habendam.**
3. **sī quis ita fēcerit, poenās dabit.**
4. **haec āiō nec quisquam negat.**
5. **bonī sunt nescioquō modō amābiliōrēs quam scelestī.**
6. Both sisters love the same boy (use uterque).
7. Sometimes she comes to Rome; but soon she will stay here for some time.
8. The general ordered every tenth man to be killed.
9. Wherever you go to, you will not avoid some bore (molestus) or other.
10. If any senator complains, I shall think about the matter again.

Some tips

| Words easily confused

adeō, adīre, adiī, aditum	I go to, approach
adeō	to such an extent, so very
aestās, aestātis, *f.*	summer
aestus, aestūs, *m.*	heat, tide, passion
aetās, aetātis, *f.*	age
audeō, audēre, ausus sum	I dare
audiō, audīre (4)	I hear
aura, aurae, *f.*	wind, breeze
auris, auris, *f.*	ear
aurum, aurī, *n.*	gold
cadō, cadere, cecidī, cāsum	I fall, befall; I am killed
occidō, occidere, occidī, occāsum	I fall down; I die
caedō, caedere, cecīdī, caesum	I cut, kill
occīdō, occīdere, occīdī, occīsum	I kill
calidus, calida, calidum	hot
callidus, callida, callidum	expert, wily
campus, campī, *m.*	plain
castra, castrōrum, *n.pl.*	camp
careō (2) + abl.	I am without, lack
carō, carnis, *f.*	flesh, meat
cārus, cāra, cārum	dear
cōnsistō, cōnsistere, cōnstitī, cōnstitum	I stop, stand
cōnstituō, cōnstituere, cōnstituī, cōnstitūtum	I decide, place in position
eques, equitis, *m.*	horseman
equus, equī, *m.*	horse
fretum, fretī, *n.*	strait, sea
frētus, frēta, frētum + abl.	relying on

gena, genae, *f.*	cheek
gener, generī, *m.*	son-in-law
generōsus, generōsa, generōsum	noble
genetrīx, genetrīcis, *f.*	mother
genitor, genitōris, *m.*	father
gēns, gentis, *f.*	race, people
genū, genūs, *n.*	knee
genus, generis, *n.*	birth, nationality
gignō, gignere, genuī, genitum	I give birth to, beget
iaceō, iacēre, iacuī	I lie
iaciō, iacere, iēcī, iactum	I throw
iactō (1)	I throw; I boast (of)
iter, itineris, *n.*	journey
iterum	again
lateō, latēre, latuī	I lie hidden, escape notice
lātus, lāta, lātum	wide
latus, lateris, *n.*	side
liber, librī, *m.*	book
līber, lībera, līberum	free
līberī, līberōrum, *m.pl.*	children
lībertus, lībertī, *m.*	freedman, ex-slave
mālō, mālle, māluī	I prefer
malum, malī, *n.*	evil, misfortune
malus, mala, malum	bad
mālum, mālī, *n.*	apple
mālus, mālī, *m.*	mast of a ship
mālus, mālī, *f.*	apple-tree

☑ **Note:**

This ditty is sung in *The Turn of the Screw, the opera by Benjamin Britten and Myfanwy Piper. According to Piper, Britten himself supplied this 'from an old-fashioned Latin grammar that an aunt of mine produced'.*
Malo: I would rather be
Malo: in an apple-tree
Malo: than a naughty boy
Malo: in adversity.

manē!	wait!
māne	in the morning, early next day
maneō, manēre, mānsī, mānsum	I remain, wait, wait for
mānēs, mānium, *m.pl.*	ghosts of the dead
manus, manūs, *f.*	hand
morior, morī, mortuus sum	I die
moror, morārī, morātus sum	I delay
opera, operae, *f.*	work, labour
ops, opis, *f.*	power, help
opēs, opum, *f. pl.*	wealth, resources
opus, operis, *n.*	work, effort
cf. **onus, oneris,** *n.*	burden
opus est mihi (**tibi,** *etc.*) + abl.	I (you, etc.) need
ōra, ōrae, *f.*	sea-coast, bank
ōrō (1)	I pray
ōs, ōris, *n.*	mouth
os, ossis, *n.*	bone
pāreō, parēre, pārui + dat.	I obey
pariō, parere, peperī, partum	I give birth to, create
parō, parāre, parāuī, parātum	I prepare
pereō, perīre, periī/perīuī, peritum	I perish
pecus, pecoris, *n.*	herd, flock
pecus, pecudis, *f.*	a farm animal
porta, portae, *f.*	gate
portō, portāre, portāuī, portātum	I carry
portus, portūs, *m.*	harbour
quaerō, quaerere, quaesīuī, quaesītum	I seek
queror, querī, questus sum	I complain
quīdam, quaedam, quoddam	a certain
quidem	indeed
ratis, ratis, *f.*	raft, boat
reor, rērī, ratus sum	I think
reus, reī, *m.*	defendant
reddō, reddere, reddidī, redditum	I give back
redeō, redīre, rediī, reditum	I go back, return
rēgālis, rēgālis, rēgāle	royal
rēgia, rēgiae, *f.*	palace

rēgīna, rēgīnae, *f.*	queen
regiō, regiōnis, *f.*	region
rēgius, rēgia, rēgium	royal
rēgnō (1)	I reign
rēgnum, rēgnī, *n.*	kingdom
regō, regere, rēxī, rēctum	I rule
seruiō, seruīre, seruiī, seruītum + dat.	I serve, am a slave to
seruō, seruāre, seruāuī, seruātum	I save, preserve
sōl, sōlis, *m.*	sun
soleō, solēre, solitus sum	I am accustomed
solium, soliī, *n.*	throne
solum, solī, *n.*	soil, ground
soluō, soluere, soluī, solūtum	I loosen, untie
sōlus, sōla, sōlum	alone
sōlum	only
tamen	however
tandem	at length
uinciō, uincīre, uīnxī, uīnctum	I bind, tie
uincō, uincere, uīcī, uictum	I conquer
uīuō, uīuere, uīxī, uīctum	I live
uir, uirī, *m.*	man
uīs, *f.*	strength, force
uīrēs, uīrium, *f.pl.*	strength
uīrus, uīrī, *n.*	venom
uīta, uītae, *f.*	life
uītis, uītis, *f.*	vine, staff of vine-wood
uītō, uītāre, uītāuī, uītātum	I avoid

Some miscellaneous points

1. A famous, crisp comment by Julius Caesar proves a good way of remembering three common perfects:
   uēnī, uīdī, uīcī
   I came, I saw, I conquered

2. If you know **sum**, you also know quite a lot of **possum** (I am able, can). **possum** is the syllable **pos-** or **pot-** + **sum**. **pos-** is used when the part of

sum begins with a consonant, **pot-** is used when the part of **sum** begins with a vowel, e.g.:

pos-sum, pot-es, pot-est, pos-sumus, pot-estis, pos-sunt.

But note **potuī, potuerō**, and **potueram** (from **pot(f)uī**, etc.).

3. **post** is usually a preposition, i.e. it is usually followed by a noun or pronoun: **post merīdiem** = after midday (but note the adverbial use **tribus** *post* **annīs** = three years later); **posteā** is an adverb: **posteā montem ascendī** = afterwards I climbed the mountain); **postquam** is a conjunction: **domum reuēnī postquam meōs amīcōs uīsī** = I came back home after I had visited my friends.

   In the same way **ante** is usually a preposition (though, like **post**, it can double as an adverb), **anteā** is an adverb, and **antequam** is a conjunction.

4. **ut** + *the subjunctive*. When **ut** is followed by the subjunctive, it is almost certain to be introducing one of **only three** constructions: purpose, result, and indirect command.

5. **ut** + *the indicative* is likely to mean 'as' or 'when'.

For English into Latin

1. It is hardly ever correct to translate the word 'tell' by the Latin **dīcō**, which means 'I say'.

   I tell *you a story.*

   Here **nārrō** (1) (*I relate*) *is appropriate*:
   fābulam tibi nārrō.

   I tell you about the message.
   Here (**aliquem**) **certiōrem faciō** (*I inform*) *is appropriate*:
   dē nūntiō tē certiōrem faciō.

   I tell *you to do this.*
   Here a word for 'command' *or* 'order' *is appropriate.*
   iubeō tē hoc facere.
   imperō tibi ut hoc faciās.

2. Of the Latin words for 'I leave', **relinquō** is the only one followed by an accusative.

   I left the city *can be translated* **urbem relīquī**.

   Otherwise, **ā, ab, ē,** *or* **ex** *with the ablative will be used*:
   ab urbe exiī–ex urbe discessī.

Appendices

Roman dates

The adjectives referring to the Roman months (**mēnsis, mēnsis,** *m. month*) are:

Iānuārius	January
Februārius	February
Martius	March
Aprīlis	April
Māius	May
Iūnius	June
Iūlius (Quīnctīl-is, -e)	July (named after Julius Caesar)
Augustus (Sextīl-is, -e)	August (named after Augustus, the first Roman emperor)
September	September
Octōber	October
Nouember	November
December	December

The words ending in **-us** decline like **bonus, -a, -um**; those ending in **-er** decline like **ācer, ācris, ācre**.

The Roman year originally began on 1 March. Hence the fact that September, October, November, and December mean the 7th, 8th, 9th, and 10th month respectively. The original names for July and August meant the 5th and 6th.

Julius Caesar's reform of 46 BC in effect invented the modern year. He at last established the figure of 365 days, missing only a quarter day per year— hence the leap-year.

The three key Roman days of the month were:

Kalendae, Kalendārum, *f.pl.*	Kalends or 1st
Nōnae, Nōnārum, *f.pl.*	Nones or 5th
Īdūs, Īduum, *f.pl.*	Ides or 13th

☑ **Note:**
In March, July, October, May,
Nones is the 7th, Ides the 15th day.
Nōnae is simply the '9th' day before the Ides.

| The rules

1. If the date falls *on* one of these days, the *ablative* is used:

Īdibus Martiīs

on the Ides of March, 15 March

2. If the date falls *on the day before* one of these days, **prīdiē** + *accusative* is used:

prīdiē Īdūs Martiās

on the day before the Ides of March, i.e. *on 14 March*

3. All other dates are counted back from the next key date (Kalends, Nones, or Ides). The counting is done inclusively, i.e. including both the key date and the date referred to.

The expression **ante diem** + the appropriate ordinal number (i.e. **prīmus, secundus, tertius, quārtus**, etc.) agreeing with *diem* (i.e. in the accusative masculine singular) and the *accusative* of the key date with the adjective indicating the month agreeing with it (i.e. in the accusative feminine plural):

ante diem tertium Nōnās Iānuāriās

three days before the Nones of January.

In our calendar, the Nones of January are the 5th. Count 3 days back from 5 January (*including that date*) and it transpires that the Roman date referred to is 3 January.

The Roman date is frequently abbreviated to, for example, **a.d. iii Nōn. Iān.**

Give our modern equivalent of: **a.d. vi Īd. Mart.** and **a.d. v Nōn. Oct.**

4. For dates *after* the Ides, the counting has to be done from the Kalends *of the next month*. Inclusive counting will lead to the inclusion of *both* the key date and the last day of the month in which the date actually falls. Thus: **a.d. vii Kal. Apr.** is a date in *March*. In the number 7 there are included *both* 1 April (the Kalends) *and* 31 March. Counting back we thus arrive at 26 March as the modern equivalent.

If you are converting an English date into Latin, the easiest way to proceed is to add two to the number of the days in the English month (i.e. for 26 March, add 2 to 31 = 33 and subtract the modern date (33–26 = 7). Thus we arrive at vii. And the Roman date is **a.d. vii Kal. Apr.**

What is your birthday in Latin?

Roman Money

The **sēstertius** (*m.*) was the unit in which Roman money was usually counted. It was a silver coin worth 2½ **assēs** (*m.*, singular **ās, assis**). That is how it got its name: half a third, *sēmis-tertius*, i.e. 2½. The **dēnārius** (*m.*), also a silver coin, was worth four *sēstertiī* (*sesterces* in English). The **aureus**, a gold coin first minted by Julius Caesar, was originally worth 25 *dēnāriī*, but later its value declined. Coins below the value of the *sēstertius* were made of copper.

Sums up to 2,000 sesterces were given as one would expect: the cardinal number with the plural of *sēstertius*: **trecentī sēstertiī** = *three hundred sesterces*.

For sums from 2,000 to 1,000,000 sesterces, the word **sēstertia** (*n.pl.*) was used to mean 'a thousand sesterces' with distributive numerals (1–10: **singulī, -ae, -a; bīnī; ternī; quaternī; quīnī; sēnī; septēnī; octōnī, nouēnī, dēnī**): **terna sēstertia** = *three thousand sesterces*.

For sums of 1,000,000 and above, the word **sēstertium** (*gen. plur.*) was used with adverbial numbers (*semel, bis, ter, etc.*). **sēstertium** has the meaning 'a hundred thousand sesterces'. Thus **ūndeciēs sēstertium** = *1,100,000 sesterces*.

Abbreviations

The word *sēstertius* is abbreviated to HS (the H is made up of II joined together, while the S stands for *sēmis* (half), i.e. 2½ (*assēs*)).

The word *sēstertia* is abbreviated to HS. A line is placed above the numeral: **HS $\overline{\text{XIV}}$** = *14,000 sesterces*.

sēstertium is abbreviated to HS with a line over the letters as well as the numeral: **$\overline{\text{HS}}$ $\overline{\text{XIV}}$** = *1,400,000 sesterces*. This can also be written **HS $\boxed{\text{XIV}}$**.

Roman weights and measures

Weights

The **lībra** (*f.*) or **ās** (*m.*), three quarters of a modern pound or 327 grams, was divided into 12 **ūnciae** (an **ūncia** was 27.3 grams, almost exactly the same weight as a modern ounce). The other units were a **sextāns** (a sixth of the lībra, 54.6 grams), **quadrāns** or **terūncius** (a quarter, 81.8 grams), **triēns** (109 grams—a quarter of a modern pound), **quīncūnx** (136 grams), **sēmis** (164 grams), **septūnx** (191 grams), **bēs** (218 grams—half a modern pound), **dōdrāns** (245 grams), **dēxtāns** (273 grams), and **deūnx** (300 grams).

Lengths

The **pēs** (*m.*) was very slightly less than a modern foot (30 cm, 0.971 feet). A **passus** (*m.*) was 5 Roman feet (1.48 metres, 4.85 feet). The mile (**mīlle passūs**) consisted of 1,000 Roman feet (1480 metres, 1.48 kilometres—4850 feet, $\frac{9}{10}$ of a modern mile).

A **iūgerum** (*n.*) was a measure of land 240 × 120 Roman feet, $\frac{5}{8}$ of an English acre (1.544 hectares).

Roman names

Distinguished Romans had at least three names: the **praenōmen**, the individual name; the **nōmen**, the name of the **gēns** (the clan); and the **cognōmen**, the name of the family within the *gēns*. Thus Gāius Iūlius Caesar is *Gāius* of the *gēns Iūlia* and the *Caesar* family.

All Roman citizens had a *praenōmen* and the name of their *gēns*.

The most common *praenōmina* were abbreviated as follows:

A.	Aulus
C.	Cāius *or* Gāius[1]
Cn.	Gnaeus[1]
D.	Decimus
L.	Lūcius
M.	Marcus
M'.	Mānius
P.	Pūblius
Q.	Quīntus
S. (Sex.)	Sextus
Ser.	Seruius
Sp.	Spurius
T.	Titus
Ti. (Tib.)	Tiberius

••••➤ 1. The early Latin alphabet had no separate sign for 'g'.

☑ **Note:**

The Latin for 'Tom, Dick and Harry' is **Gāiusque Lūciusque**.

Some Literary Terms

alliteration   the recurrence of the same consonant (cf. *assonance*), especially at the beginning of words or syllables–**ēripite hanc pestem perniciemque mihi** (snatch away this plague and destruction from me)–Catullus, 76.20. The use of alliteration imparts emphasis, and the effect this creates depends on the meaning of the words emphasized.

anacoluthon   a sentence which lacks grammatical sequence, i.e. in which one construction stops and another starts before the former is completed–**mē, mē, adsum quī fēcī, in mē conuertite ferrum** (me, me, I am here, the man who did the deed, turn your swords on me)–Virgil, *Aeneid*, 9.427.

anaphora   the repetition of a word or phrase in several successive clauses–**nihil uērī, nihil sānctī, nūllus deum metus, nūllum iūs iūrandum, nūlla rēligiō** (no truth, no sanctity, no fear of the gods, no standing by oaths, no religion)–Livy, 21.4.9.

antithesis   the contrasting of ideas emphasized by the arrangement of words–**ōdī et amō** (I hate and I love)–Catullus, 85.1.

aposiopesis   a device in which the speaker breaks off before completing the sentence–Neptune breaks off his threats to the winds and calms the sea: **quōs ego . . . sed mōtōs praestat compōnere fluctūs** ((you winds) which I . . . But calming the disturbed waves takes precedence)–Virgil, *Aeneid*, 1.135.

apostrophe   the writer 'turns away from' his narrative (told in the third person) to address one of his characters. Thus at *Aeneid*, 4.408–12, Virgil addresses first Dido and then the god Amor (Love).

assonance   the occurrence of similar vowel sounds in words close to each other (cf. *alliteration*)–**lītus ut *longē resonante Eōā tunditur undā*** (where the beach is pounded by the far-echoing Eastern wave)–Catullus, 11.3–4.

asyndeton   the omission of conjunctions (such as 'and' or 'but') where these would usually occur–**clāmor, lapidēs, fustēs, gladiī** (shouting, stones, clubs, swords)–Cicero, *ad Atticum*, 4.3.3.

bathos   the juxtaposition of the intense or important and the trivial–**parturiunt montēs; nāscētur rīdiculus mūs** (the mountains are in labour, and there will be born a comical mouse)–Horace, *Ars Poetica*, 139.

chiasmus a pair of balanced phrases where the order of the second reverses that of the first–**haec queritur, stupet haec** (this woman complains, this one gapes)–Ovid, *Ars Amatoria*, 1.124.

closure the sense of completion or resolution at the conclusion of a literary work or part of a literary work. Often these conclusions *deny* us this sense of completion, as at the end of Virgil's *Aeneid* when the pious hero's frenzied brutality is seen by many as a violation of the civilized values which the poem has established.

deixis (*adjective* **deictic**) the use of words or expressions to *point* to some feature of a situation. Pronouns (e.g. **ego, tū** (I, you), etc.) and words of place (**hīc, illīc** (here, there), etc.) and time (**iam, tum** (now, then), etc.) tell us such things about a situation as who is involved in it, and where or when it takes place.

ellipsis the shortening of a sentence or phrase by the omission of words which can be understood–**quid plūra?** (why (should I say) more?)–Cicero, *Philippic*, 8.5.1.

enallage and **hypallage** (in practice these terms cannot be distinguished) the use of the transferred epithet, i.e. transferring an adjective from the word to which it properly applies to another word in the same phrase–**Lātōnae tacitum pertemptant gaudia pectus** (joy thrills the silent heart of Latona)–Virgil, *Aeneid*, 1.502. It is Latona who is silent, not her heart (which cannot speak). An example of double enallage is **ībant obscūrī sōlā sub nocte** (they went dark beneath the lonely night) Virgil, *Aeneid*, 6.268. R.G. Austin comments: 'Virgil's arrangement brings out, with great impact on the reader, the dim groping figures in a terrifying loneliness of night.'

enjambement running a sentence over the end of a line of verse and then ending it after the first word of the new line, lending emphasis to that word–**sōla domō maeret uacuā strātīsque relictīs/incubat** (she grieves alone in her house and on the couch he has left she lies down)–Virgil, *Aeneid*, 4.82–3.

epanalepsis the repetition of a word after a number of other words–**mē patriīs āuectam, perfide, ab ārīs, perfide . . .?** (you traitor, (did you) take me away from my ancestral altars, you traitor . . .?)–Catullus, 64, 132–3.

euphemism the substitution of a mild or roundabout expression for one considered improper or too harsh or blunt–**anagnōstēs noster dēcesserat** (my reading-slave had departed (this life), i.e. died)–Cicero, *ad Atticum*, 1.12.4.

hendiadys   a single idea expressed through two nouns–**paterīs lībāmus et aurō** (*literally*, we pour from bowls and gold, *but meaning* we pour from golden bowls)–Virgil, *Georgics*, 2.192.

hyperbaton   the arbitrary dislocation of normal word order, by way of displacing one part of one clause into another–**tussim,/nōn immerentī quam mihī meus uenter,/dum sumptuōsās appetō, dedit, cēnās** (a cough which–serves me right!–my stomach, while I hankered after lavish dinners, gave me)–Catullus, 44.7–9. It is impossible to reproduce in English the violence done here to a natural Latin word order.

hyperbole   the use of exaggerated terms, not to be taken literally–**uirginitās mīlle petīta procīs** (virginity sought by a thousand suitors, i.e. a large number of suitors)–Ovid, *Heroides*, 16.104.

hysteron proteron   the reversal of the normal (temporal) order of events–at *Aeneid*, 4.154–5, Virgil writes that the animals career over the plains and leave the mountains. Obviously they leave the mountains before they career over the plains. By his order Virgil lays emphasis on what he describes first, which seems to him the more important action. Ovid uses **redit itque** (he returns and he goes) (e.g. at *Metamorphoses*, 2.509) to mean 'he goes and returns'. This reflects the fact that the Latin sentence, unlike the English, is arranged in a circle.

irony   the expression of one's meaning by using words of the opposite meaning in order to make one's remarks forceful–perhaps Catullus' high praise of Cicero–he calls him the most eloquent of Romans, past, present and future (49.1–3)–falls into this category.

juxtaposition   the placing of words next to each other for effect (cf. *oxymoron*)–**illum absēns absentem audit** (she hears him when he is not here when she is away from him)–Virgil, *Aeneid*, 4.83.

liminality   the use of location, especially involving passing through doors or gates, to make a symbolic point–Dido and Aeneas set out from the palace in the civilized orderly city and go into the wild woods where a fearsome storm rages and chaos erupts (Virgil, *Aeneid*, 4.135–72).

litotes   the use of understatement, involving a negative, to emphasize one's meaning (the opposite of *hyperbole*)–**fōrmaque nōn tacitī funeris intus erat** (and inside there was the appearance of a not-quiet, i.e. noisy funeral)–Ovid, *Tristia*, 1.3.22.

metaphor   the application of a word or phrase to something it does not apply to literally, indicating a comparison–**tuō lepōre incēnsus** (set on fire by your charm)–Catullus, 50.7–8. The poet has not been literally set on fire.

metonymy a form of expression by which a person or thing takes his, her, or its name from something which they are associated with–Ovid uses the word 'forum' to refer to the law courts located there; **cēdant arma togae** (literally, let arms give way to the toga) means 'let war give way to peace' (Cicero, *Poems*, fragment 11); the name Mars, the god of war, can be used simply to mean 'war', just as that of Ceres, the goddess of fertility, can be used to mean 'bread' or 'food' (as at Virgil, *Aeneid*, 1.177, where it is applied to waterlogged grain).

onomatopoeia words or combinations of words, the sound of which suggests their sense–*tintinnant* **aurēs**(my ears ring)–Catullus, 51.11. A famous example is **at tuba terribilī sonitū taratantara dīxit** (but the trumpet said 'taratantara' with a fearful sound) Ennius, *Annals*, 140.

oxymoron the juxtaposition (see entry) of two words of contradictory meaning to emphasize the contradiction–**concordia discors** (a discordant harmony)–Lucan, *Bellum Ciuile*, 1.98.

paradox a statement which apparently contradicts itself but in fact makes a meaningful point–a Scottish chieftain denounces Roman imperialism: **ubi sōlitūdinem faciunt pācem appellant** (where they make a desert, they call it peace)–Tacitus, *Agricola*, 30.6.

paronomasia a punning play on words–**Libycīs teris ōtia terrīs** (you waste time in the Libyan lands)–Virgil, *Aeneid*, 4.271.

parse to describe a word grammatically–e.g. **amās** is the second person singular of the present indicative active of **amō**, a first conjugation verb meaning 'I love'.

periphrasis a circumlocutory way of saying things–Ovid tells us that his brother was four times three (*tribus . . . quater*) months older than himself, i.e. one year older–*Tristia*, 4.10.10. In fact this periphrasis is necessary in a dactylic line: **duodecim** (twelve) won't scan.

personification the representation of an idea or thing as having human characteristics–as in Catullus, 4, where a yacht speaks.

pleonasm the use of unnecessary words–**sīc ōre locūta est** (thus she spoke from her mouth)–Virgil, *Aeneid*, 1.614.

polyptoton the repetition of a word in a different form/case–**uxor amāns flentem flēns ācrius ipsa tenēbat** (my loving wife, weeping more bitterly herself, embraced me as I wept)–Ovid, *Tristia*, 1.3.17.

simile a figure of speech in which one thing is compared explicitly to another–see Virgil, where, in one of many similes, the Carthaginians are likened to bees (*Aeneid*, 1.430-5). The simile is a notable feature of epic–hence 'epic simile'.

syllepsis an expression in which the same verb is used in two different senses, literal and metaphorical (contrast *zeugma*)–**fugam Dīdō sociōsque parābat** (Dido prepared flight and companions)–the word 'prepared' means something different with each of its objects–Virgil, *Aeneid*, 1.360. This is Ovid's favourite literary device. See e.g. **dēpositō pariter cum ueste timōre** (my fear put aside together with my dress)–*Heroides*, 18.55.

synecdoche a form of expression is which the part in used to imply the whole–Dido uses the word 'keels' (**carīnae**) to refer to whole ships–Virgil, *Aeneid*, 4.658.

tautology repeating the same thing in different ways–**sōla domō . . . uacuā** (alone in (her) empty house)–Virgil, *Aeneid*, 4.82.

tricolon the use of three parallel clauses, phrases, or words–**rētia rara, plagae, lātō uēnābula ferrō** (wide-meshed nets, trap-nets, broad-bladed hunting-spears)–Virgil, *Aeneid*, 4. 131.

tricolon auctum or **crescendo** the use of three parallel clauses or phrases which build to a climax, the last element usually being the longest–**sed rēgīna tamen, sed opācī maxima mundī,/sed tamen īnfernī pollēns mātrōna tyrannī** (but still (she was) a queen, the great queen of the world of shadows, still the mighty consort of the king of the underworld)–Ovid, *Metamorphoses*, 5.507-8.

zeugma a figure of speech in which a verb or adjective is applied to two nouns, though it is literally applicable to only one of them, e.g. 'with tearful eyes and mind' (contrast *syllepsis*). **longa tibi exsilia et uastum maris aequor arandum** (a long exile and a vast expanse of sea must be ploughed by you)–Virgil, *Aeneid*, 2.780. The metaphor of ploughing is appropriate to the idea of effortfully crossing the sea, but the notion of exile cries out for a different word, and some violence is done to the language. Formally, it is incorrect writing.

Vocabulary: Latin–English

- This vocabulary covers Latin examples and practice sentences.
- Nouns are given with their genitive singular and gender, adjectives in their masculine, feminine and neuter forms in the nominative singular, and verbs with their principal parts or conjugation.
- 1st conjugation words follow the pattern of **amō, amāre, amāuī, amātum**.
- 2nd conjugation words follow the pattern of **moneō, monēre, monuī, monitum**.
- 4th conjugation words follow the pattern of **audiō, audīre, audīuī, audītum**.

ā *or* **ab** + abl.	by, from
abeō, abīre, abiī or **abīuī, abitum**	I go away
abripiō, abripere, abripuī, abreptum	I steal, snatch away
absum, abesse, āfuī	I am absent, I am distant
accēdō, accēdere, accessī, accessum	I approach, go to
accidit, accidere, accidit ut + subj.	it happens that
accipiō, accipere, accēpī, acceptum	I receive, hear
accūsō (1)	I accuse
ācer, ācris, ācre (adverb **ācriter**)	keen, furious
aciēs, aciēī, *f.*	battle formation, army
ad + acc.	to
adeō	to such an extent
adeō, adīre, adiī or **adiīuī, aditum**	I go to
adiuuō, adiuuāre, adiūuī, adiūtum	I help
admittō, admittere, admīsī, admissum	I commit, grant
admoneō (2)	I advise, warn
adsum, adesse, adfuī	I am present
adueniō, aduenīre, aduēnī, aduentum	I arrive
aduentus, aduentūs, *m.*	arrival
aduersārius, aduersāriī, *m.*	opponent, enemy
aedificō (1)	I build
aeger, aegra, aegrum	sick
ager, agrī, *m.*	field
agō, agere, ēgī, āctum	I do, drive

āiō	I say
aliquī, aliquae, aliquod	some, any
aliquis, aliquis, aliquid	someone, something
amābilis, amābilis, amābile	likeable
amātor, amātōris, *m.*	lover
ambō, ambae, ambō	both
ambulō (1)	I walk
amīca, amīcae, *f.*	girlfriend
amīcus, amīcī, *m.*	friend
āmittō, āmittere, āmīsī, āmissum	I lose, dismiss
amō (1)	I love
animus, animī, *m.*	mind, character
annus, annī, *m.*	year
ante + acc.	before
anteā	before
antequam	before
ānxius, ānxia, ānxium	anxious
appropinquō (1) + dat.	approach
arbitror, arbitrārī, arbitrātus sum	I think, observe
argentum, argentī, *n.*	silver, money
arma, armōrum, *n.pl.*	arms
ars, artis, *f.*	art
astrum, astrī, *n.*	star
Athēnae, Athēnārum, *f.pl.*	Athens
auctor, auctōris, *m.* or *f.*	maker, author, finder, instigator
auctōritās, auctōritātis, *f.*	authority
audiō (4)	I hear, listen
autem (*2nd word*)	but, however, moreover
auxilium, auxiliī, *n.*	help
bellum, bellī, *n.*	war
bēstia, bēstiae, *f.*	beast, wild beast
bonus, bona, bonum	good
Britannī, Britannōrum, *m.pl.*	the Britons
Britannia, Britanniae, *f.*	Britain
Brundisium, Brundisiī, *n.*	Brundisium
Caesar, Caesaris	Caesar
campus, campī, *m.*	plain
canis, canis, *m.* or *f.*	dog
captīuus, captīuī, *m.*	prisoner, captive

caput, capitis, *n.*	head, life
careō (2) + abl.	I am without, want, lack
carmen, carminis, *n.*	song, poem
caueō, cauēre, cāuī, cautum	I am on my guard (against), beware
causa, causae, *f.*	cause
celer, celeris, celere (*adverb* **celeriter**)	fast, swift
cēlō (1)	I hide
cēna, cēnae, *f.*	dinner, meal
certē	certainly
certiōrem faciō, facere, fēcī, factum (see pp. 84 & 141)	I inform
cīuis, cīuis, *m.* or *f.*	citizen
clārus, clāra, clārum	clear, bright, famous, illustrious
claudō, claudere, clausī, clausum	I shut
cognōscō, cognōscere, cognōuī, cognitum	I get to know
collis, collis, *m.*	hill
colō, colere, coluī, cultum	I revere, cultivate, inhabit
commūniō (4)	I fortify
concidō, concidere, concidī	I fall, am killed
cōnficiō, cōnficere, cōnfēcī, cōnfectum	I complete, finish off
cōnfiteor, cōnfitērī, cōnfessus sum	I confess, reveal
congregō (1)	I gather together
cōnscendō, cōnscendere, cōnscendī, cōnscēnsum	I get on, embark on, mount
cōnseruō (1)	I preserve, maintain
cōnsilium, cōnsiliī, *n.*	advice, plan
cōnsistō, cōnsistere, cōnstitī, cōnstitum	I stand, halt, stop
cōnspiciō, cōnspicere, cōnspexī, cōnspectum	I catch sight of, notice
cōnstituō, cōnstituere, cōnstituī, cōnstitūtum	I decide, appoint
cōnsul, cōnsulis, *m.*	consul
cōnsulō, cōnsulere, cōnsuluī, cōnsultum + dat.	I consult the interests of …
contemnō, contemnere, contempsī, contemptum	I scorn
contentus, contenta, contentum	content
cōntiō, cōntiōnis, *f.*	speech, assembly, meeting
coquus, coquī, *m.*	cook
cottīdiē	every day
crēdō, crēdere, crēdidī, crēditum + dat.	I believe, trust
cubō, cubāre, cubuī, cubitum	I lie down, sleep
culpō (1)	blame
cum	when, since, although

cum + abl.	with
cūnctor, cūnctārī, cūnctātus sum	I delay
cūria, cūriae, *f.*	senate house
cūrō (1)	I take care of, worry about
currō, currere, cucurrī, cursum	I run
currus, currūs, *m.*	chariot
damnō (1)	I condemn
dē + abl.	about, concerning
dēbellō (1)	I conquer, subdue
dēbeō (2)	I ought, owe
dēfendō, dēfendere, dēfendī, dēfēnsum	I defend
dēfessus, dēfessa, dēfessum	exhausted
dēlectō (1)	I delight
dēleō, dēlēre, dēlēuī, dēlētum	I destroy
dēterreō (2)	I deter, discourage
deus, deī, *m.*	god
dīcō, dīcere, dīxī, dictum	I say
dictātor, dictātōris, *m.*	dictator
dictum, dictī, *n.*	word, saying
diēs, diēī, *m.*	day
dignitās, dignitātis, *f.*	dignity, honour
dignus, digna, dignum	worthy
dīligēns, dīligēns, dīligēns (*adverb* **dīligenter**)	diligent, hard, careful
dīligō, dīligere, dīlēxī, dīlēctum	I hold dear, esteem highly
dīmittō, dīmittere, dīmīsī, dīmissum	I send away, dismiss
discēdō, discēdere, discessī, discessum	I depart
disertus, diserta, disertum	skilled in speaking
discipulus, discipulī, *m.*	pupil, student
distō, distāre	I am distant
diū	for a long time
dō, dare, dedī, datum	I give
doceō, docēre, docuī, doctum	I teach
doleō (2)	I grieve (at), I am in pain
dolor, dolōris, *m.*	grief, pain
dolus, dolī, *m.*	trick, trickery, treachery
domus, domī or **domūs**, *f.*	house, home
dōnō (1)	I present
dōnum, dōnī, *n.*	gift
dormiō (4)	I sleep
dubitō (1)	I doubt, hesitate
dubius, dubia, dubium	doubtful

dulcis, dulcis, dulce	sweet, pleasant, delightful
dum	while, until, provided that
dux, ducis, *m.* or *f.*	leader, guide, general
ē or **ex**	out of, from
edō, ēsse, ēdī, ēsum	I eat
effugiō, effugere, effūgī	I flee from, escape
ego	I
ēgredior, ēgredī, ēgressus sum	I go out, depart
ēiciō, ēicere, ēiēcī, ēiectum	I throw out
ēloquēns, ēloquēns, ēloquēns (*gen.* **ēloquentis**)	eloquent, articulate
emō, emere, ēmī, ēmptum	I buy
eō	to that place
eō, īre, iī or **īuī, itum**	I go
epistula, epistulae, *f.*	letter
equitātus, equitātūs, *m.*	cavalry
errō (1)	I wander, make a mistake, err
ērumpo, ērumpere, ērūpī, ēruptum	I break out, burst out, break out of
ēsuriō (4)	I am hungry
et	and, also, even
etiam	even, also
etsī	although, even if
ēuertō, ēuertere, ēuertī, ēuersum	I turn upside down, ruin
excēdō, excēdere, excessī, excessum	I go out
excipiō, excipere, excēpī, exceptum	I receive, sustain
exeō, exīre, exiī or **exīuī, exitum**	I go out
exercitus, exercitūs, *m.*	army
expellō, expellere, expulī, expulsum	I drive out
expers, expers, expers (*gen.* **expertis**) + gen.	without, lacking in
explōrātor, explōrātōris, *m.*	scout, spy
exspectō (1)	I wait
facilis, facilis, facile	easy
faciō, facere, fēcī, factum	I do, make
factum, factī, *n.*	deed
fācundus, fācunda, fācundum	eloquent
faueō, fauēre, fāuī, fautum + dat.	I favour
fēlēs, fēlis, *f.*	cat
fēmina, fēminae, *f.*	woman
ferē	almost, generally speaking
ferō, ferre, tulī, lātum	I carry, bring, endure

fessus, fessa, fessum — tired
fīdēlis, fīdēlis, fīdēle — faithful
fīlia, fīliae, *f.* — daughter
fīlius, fīliī, *m.* — son
fīō, fierī, factus sum — I happen, become
flūmen, flūminis, *n.* — river
focus, focī, *m.* — hearth
fōns, fontis, *m.* — spring, fountain, source
forte — by chance
fortis, fortis, forte — strong, brave
forum, forī, *n.* — forum, market, city centre
frāter, frātris, *m.* — brother
frequenter — often, frequently
fruor, fruī, frūctus or **fruitus sum** + abl. — I enjoy
fugiō, fugere, fūgī — I flee (from), I run away (from)
fūr, fūris, *m.* or *f.* — thief

gaudeō, gaudēre, gāuīsus sum — I rejoice, am glad
gemma, gemmae, *f.* — jewel
genus, generis, *n.* — race, birth
gerō, gerere, gessī, gestum — I carry on, deal with, wage
gladius, gladiī, *m.* — sword
Graecia, Graeciae, *f.* — Greece
grammatica, grammaticae, *f.* — grammar
grātia, grātiae, *f.* — gratitude, good will, thanks, favour
grauis, grauis, graue — heavy, serious, grievous
gubernāculum, gubernāculī, *n.* — the steering-oar, management

habeō (2) — I have; I consider; I deliver
habitō (1) — I live (in), inhabit
haud — not
Heluētiī, Heluētiōrum, *m.pl.* — the Helvetii (the Swiss)
herba, herbae, *f.* — grass
hic, haec, hoc — this
Hispānia, Hispāniae, *f.* — Spain
Homērus, Homērī, *m.* — Homer
homō, hominis, *m.* — man, human being
hōra, hōrae, *f.* — hour
hortor (1) — I encourage
hostēs, hostium, *m.pl.* — the enemy
hostis, hostis, *m.* or *f.* — enemy
hūc — over here, to here, hither

iam	now, already
iānua, iānuae, *f.*	door
idcircō	for this reason
igitur (2nd word)	therefore
ignārus, ignāra, ignārum + gen.	ignorant (of)
ignāuus, ignāua, ignāuum	idle, cowardly
ignōscō, ignōscere, ignōuī, ignōtum + dat.	I forgive
ille, illa, illud	he, she it, that, the well-known
immineō, imminēre + dat.	I threaten
impediō (4)	I hinder
impendeō, impendēre, -, impēnsum	I hang over, threaten
imperātor, imperātōris, *m.*	general
imperō (1) + dat.	I order
impetus, impetūs, *m.*	attack
in + abl.	in
in + acc.	to, into
incendō, incendere, incendī, incēnsum	I set fire to
inceptum, inceptī, *n.*	undertaking, beginning
incipiō, incipere, incēpī, inceptum	I begin
indignus, indigna, indignum	unworthy
ineō, inīre, iniī or **iniuī, initum**	I go into
ingredior, ingredī, ingressus sum	I go into
īnsāniō (4)	I am crazy
intellegō, intellegere, intellēxī, intellēctum	I understand
interest	it makes a difference, it matters
interficiō, interficere, interfēcī, interfectum	I kill
intrō (1)	I enter
inueniō, inuenīre, inuēnī, inuentum	I find
inuītus, inuīta, inuītum	unwilling
ipse, ipsa, ipsum	himself, herself, itself
īrātus, īrāta, īrātum	angry
is, ea, id	he, she, it, this
iste, ista, istud	that
ita	in such a way, like this
iter, itineris, *n.*	journey, travel
iubeō, iubēre, iussī, iussum	I order
iūcundus, iūcunda, iūcundum	pleasant, agreeable
iūrō (1)	I swear
iūstus, iūsta, iūstum	just

iuxtā + acc.	near
labor, labōris, *m.*	labour, toil, hardship
labōrō (1)	I work
lacus, lacūs, *m.*	lake
laedō, laedere, laesī, laesum	I hurt
laetus, laeta, laetum	happy
lapis, lapidis, *m.*	stone
lātus, lāta, lātum	wide, broad
laudō (1)	I praise
lautus, lauta, lautum	fashionable, clean
lēgātus, lēgātī, *m.*	legate, ambassador, commander
legō, legere, lēgī, lēctum	I gather, read
lentus, lenta, lentum	slow
leō, leōnis, *m.*	lion
lēx, lēgis, *f.*	law
libenter	gladly, willingly
līber, lībera, līberum	free
liber, librī, *m.*	book
līberī, līberōrum, *m.pl.*	children
līberō (1)	I free
licet (see p. 128)	it is allowed, even though
licet mihi, licēre mihi, licuit mihi, licitum est mihi (see p. 104)	I am allowed
Ligus, Liguris, *m.*	a Ligurian (from Cisalpine Gaul)
litterae, litterārum, *f.pl.*	literature, a letter
locus, locī, *m.*	place
loquor, loquī, locūtus sum	I speak, talk, say
lūdō, lūdere, lūsī, lūsum	I play, trick
lūx, lūcis, *f.*	light
magnopere	greatly
magnus, magna, magnum	great, big
māiestās, māiestātis, *f.*	majesty, treason
malus, mala, malum	bad, evil
maneō, manēre, mānsī, mānsum	I stay, wait, wait for
mare, maris, *n.*	sea
marītus, marītī, *m.*	husband
maximus, maxima, maximum	very great, greatest, very big
mē	me, *acc. of* ego
melior, melior, melius	better
meminī, meminisse	I remember

memoria, memoriae, *f.*	memory
mendāx, mendāx, mendāx (*gen.* **mendācis**)	lying, false
mēnsa, mēnsae, *f.*	table
mereor, merērī, meritus sum	deserve
merīdiē	at midday
metuō, metuere, metuī, metūtum	I am afraid (of), I fear (to)
meus, mea, meum	my
mīles, mīlitis, *m.*	soldier
mīlle passūs, mīlle passuum, *m.pl.*	a mile
mīlia passuum, *n.pl.*	miles
minimum	very little
minimus, minima, minimum	very small, very little, least
minor, minārī, minātus sum	I threaten
miser, misera, miserum	unhappy, wretched
miseret (mē) (see p. 105)	I am sorry for
mittō, mittere, mīsī, missum	I send
modus, modī, *m.*	way, manner, limit
moenia, moenium, *n.pl.*	city walls
molestus, molesta, molestum	annoying, boring
mōmentum, mōmentī, *n.*	importance
moneō (2)	I advise, I warn
morior, morī, mortuus sum	I die
mors, mortis, *f.*	death
mōs, mōris, *m.*	custom, civilization
moueō, mouēre, mōuī, mōtum	I move
mox	soon
multō	much
multum	much
mūrus, mūrī, *m.*	wall
mūs, mūris, *m.*	mouse
nārrō (1)	I tell, narrate
nāscor, nāscī, nātus sum	I am born
nātālis, nātālis, *m.*	birthday
nāuigō (1)	I sail
nāuis, nāuis, *f.*	ship
nauta, nautae, *m.*	sailor
nec	and ... not
nec/neque	and not
necō (1)	I kill
negō (1)	I say ... not, deny, refuse, say no

nēmō, nēminis, *m.* or *f.*	no one, nobody
neque iam	and no longer
neque/nec	and not
nesciō (4)	I do not know
nescioquō modō	in some way
neu/nēue	and don't, and not
nēue/neu	and don't, and not
nihil, *n.*	nothing
nihilum, nihilī, *n.*	nothing
ningit, ningere, nīnxit	it snows
nisi	unless, if not
nōlō, nōlle, nōluī	I am unwilling, refuse
nōn	not
nōn iam	no longer
nōn modo ... sed etiam	not only ... but also
nōn quō/nōn quod	not because
nōndum	not yet
nōnnūllī, nōnnūllōrum, *m.pl.*	some (people)
nōnus, nōna, nōnum	ninth
nōs	we
nostrī, nostrōrum, *m.pl.*	our men
nox, noctis, *f.*	night
nūllus, nūlla, nūllum	not any, no
numquam	never
nunc	now
nūntiō (1)	I announce
nūntius, nūntiī, *m.*	news, messenger
ob + acc.	on account of
obdūrō (1)	I persist, endure
oblīuīscor, oblīuīscī, oblītus sum + gen.	I forget
obses, obsidis, *m.* or *f.*	hostage
obsideō, obsidēre, obsēdī, obsessum	I besiege, picket
obstō, obstāre, obstitī, obstātum + dat.	stand in the way (of)
obuiam + dat.	to meet
occāsus, occāsūs, *m.*	setting
occidō, occidere, occidī, occāsum	I set, fall down, die
occīdō, occīdere, occīdī, occīsum	I kill
ōdī, ōdisse	I hate
offendō, offendere, offendī, offēnsum	I offend, displease
omnis, omnis, omne	every, all

oportet, oportēre, oportuit — it is my duty, it is necessary

oppidum, oppidī, *n.* — town
oppugnō (1) — I attack
optimus, optima, optimum — the best, very good
ōrātiō, ōrātiōnis, *f.* — speech
ōrātor, ōrātōris, *m.* — speaker, orator
ōrdō, ōrdinis, *m.* — rank
ōrō (1) — I beg, pray to
ōtium, ōtiī, *n.* — leisure, ease

paenitet mē (see p. 105) — I am sorry for, I repent
pandō, pandere, pandī, pānsum or **passum** — I open, spread out, reveal
pār, pār, pār (*gen.* **paris)** — equal, fair
parātus, parāta, parātum — prepared
parcō, parcere, pepercī + dat. — I spare, pardon
parēns, parentis, *m.* or *f.* — parent
pāreō, pārēre, pāruī + dat. — I obey
parō (1) — I prepare
pater, patris, *m.* — father
patria, patriae, *f.* — fatherland
paucī, paucae, pauca — few
pauper, pauper, pauper (*gen.* **pauperis)** — poor
pāx, pācis, *f.* — peace
pecūnia, pecūniae, *f.* — money
pellō, pellere, pepulī, pulsum — I push, strike, defeat
perferō, perferre, pertulī, perlātum — I endure, undergo, carry through

perīculum, perīculī, *n.* — danger
perītus, perīta, perītum — skilled (in), expert (in)
persuādeō, persuādēre, persuāsī, persuāsum + dat. — I persuade
perueniō, peruenīre, peruēnī, peruentum — I arrive
pēs, pedis, *m.* — foot
petō, petere, petīuī, petītum — I seek, look, ask for
pietās, pietātis, *f.* — piety, dutifulness, love
placeō (2) + dat. — I please
plēbēs, plēbis, *f.* — common people
plūrimī, plūrimae, plūrima — very many
plūs, plūris, *n.* — more
poenam persoluō, persoluere, persoluī, persolūtum — I pay the penalty

poenās (poenam) dō, dare, dedī, datum	I pay the penalty
poēta, poētae, *m.*	poet
pōns, pontis, *m.*	bridge
porta, portae, *f.*	gate
poscō, poscere, poposcī	I ask for, demand
possum, posse, potuī	I am able, I can
post + acc.	after
postquam	after
postrīdiē	on the next day
praeda, praedae, *f.*	booty
praedīcō, praedīcere, praedīxī, praedictum	I declare, announce
praesidium, praesidiī, *n.*	help, protection, garrison
praeter modum	exceptionally
pretiōsus, pretiōsa, pretiōsum	valuable
pretium, pretiī, *n.*	price, value
prīmā lūce	at first light, at dawn
prīmus, prīma, prīmum	first
prīnceps, prīncipis, *m.*	chief man, emperor
priusquam	before
prō + abl.	on behalf of
probitās, probitātis, *f.*	honesty
procāx, procāx, procāx (*gen.* **procācis**)	pushing, impudent
prōcēdo, prōcēdere, prōcessī, prōcessum	I go forward, make progress
procul	far away
prōdeō, prōdīre, prōdiī, prōditum	I come forward
prōdō, prōdere, prōdidī, prōditum	I betray, hand down
prōficiō, prōficere, prōfēcī, prōfectum	I make progress
proficīscor, proficīscī, profectus sum	I set out
prōgredior, prōgredī, prōgressus sum	I advance, go forward
prohibeō (2)	I prevent
prōmittō, prōmittere, prōmīsī, prōmissum	I promise, send out
prope + acc.	near
properō (1)	I hurry
propior, propior, propius (*gen.* **propiōris**)	nearer
proximus, proxima, proximum	nearest, next, proceeding
pudet mē, pudēre, puduit (see p. 105)	I am ashamed
pudīcus, pudīca, pudīcum	chaste, virtuous
puella, puellae, *f.*	girl
puer, puerī, *m.*	boy
pugnō (1)	I fight

pulcher, pulchra, pulchrum	beautiful
pūniō (4)	I punish
putō (1)	I think
quaerō, quaerere, quaesīuī, quaesītum	I search for, I seek for
quālis, quālis, quāle	of what kind
quam	than
quamquam	although
quamuīs	however, although
quantum	as much as
quantus, quanta, quantum	as great as, as much as, how great
quattuor	four
-que	and
quī, quae, quod	who, which
quia	because
quīdam, quaedam, quoddam	a, a certain
quiēscō, quiēscere, quiēuī, quiētum	I rest
quīnque	five
quis? quis? quid?	who? what?
quisquam, quaequam, quicquam	any, any one, any thing
quō	to which place, in order that
quod	because
quot	how many
rapiō, rapere, rapuī, raptum	I seize, snatch, plunder
ratiō, ratiōnis, *f.*	reason
recitō (1)	I recite
redeō, redīre, rediī or **redīuī, reditum**	I return
reficiō, reficere, refēcī, refectum	I repair, rebuild, restore
rēgīna, rēgīnae, *f.*	queen
regō, regere, rēxī, rēctum	I rule
relinquō, relinquere, relīquī, relictum	I leave
reliquus, reliqua, reliquum	remaining
remittō, remittere, remīsī, remissum	I send back
reor, rērī, ratus sum	I think
repente	suddenly
repetō, repetere, repetiī or **repetīuī, repetītum**	I get back, demand back
rēs, reī, *f.*	thing, the state
rēs pūblica, reī pūblicae, *f.*	state, republic
resistō, resistere, restitī + dat.	I resist

respīrō (1) — I breathe again
respondeō, respondēre, respondī, respōnsum — I reply
restituō, restituere, restituī, restitūtum — I rebuild, restore
retineō, retinēre, retinuī, retentum — I keep, maintain, hold back

reueniō, reuenīre, reuēnī, reuentum — I come back, return
rēx, rēgis, *m.* — king
rīdeō, rīdēre, rīsī, rīsum — I laugh
Rōma, Rōmae, *f.* — Rome
Rōmānus, Rōmāna, Rōmānum — Roman
rosa, rosae, *f.* — rose
rūs, rūris, *n.* — country

saltō (1) — I dance
salūs, salūtis, *f.* — safety, health, greetings
salūtō (1) — I greet
sapiēns, sapiēns, sapiēns (*gen.* **sapientis**) — wise
sapientia, sapientiae, *f.* — wisdom
scelestus, scelesta, scelestum — wicked, criminal
scelus, sceleris, *n.* — crime
sciō (4) — I know
scrībō, scrībere, scrīpsī, scrīptum — I write
sē (see p. 26) — himself, herself, itself
secundus, secunda, secundum — second, following, favourable

sed — but
sedeō, sedēre, sēdī, sessum — I sit
semper — always
senātus, senātūs, *m.* — senate
sententia, sententiae, *f.* — opinion, judgement, vote, subject

sentiō, sentīre, sēnsī, sēnsum — I feel, notice
septem — seven
septimus, septima, septimum — seventh
sequor, sequī, secūtus sum — I follow, make for
sērius — too late
serpēns, serpentis, *f.* — serpent, snake
seruō (1) — I save, preserve, look after
sērus, sēra, sērum — late
seruus, seruī, *m.* — slave
sex — six

sexāgintā	sixty
sī	if
sī nōn	if not
sīc	thus, in this way
sīcārius, sīcāriī, *m.*	assassin
Sicilia, Siciliae, *f.*	Sicily
simul atque/ac	as soon as
sine + abl.	without
sōbrius, sōbria, sōbrium	sober
sōl, sōlis, *m.*	sun
sōlis occāsū	at sunset
soleō, solēre, solitus sum + inf.	I am accustomed to
sōlum	only
somnium, somniī, *n.*	dream
soror, sorōris, *f.*	sister
sors, sortis, *f.*	lot, fate, share
speciēs, speciēī, *f.*	appearance, sight, beauty
spēlunca, spēluncae, *f.*	cave
spērō (1)	I hope
spēs, speī, *f.*	hope, expectation
stō, stare, stetī, statum	I stand (**stat** *can mean* 'it is due to …')
studeō, studēre, studuī + dat.	I devote myself to, study
studium, studiī, *n.*	study, devotion, eagerness
stultus, stulta, stultum	stupid
subeō, subīre, subiī or **subīuī, subitum**	I approach, come to mind, undergo
succurrō, succurrere, succurrī, succursum + dat.	I run to help
sum, esse, fuī	I am
superō (1)	I conquer, overcome
suus, sua, suum	his own, her own, its own, their own
taceō (2)	I am silent
tālis, tālis, tāle	such
tam	so
tamen *(2nd word)*	nevertheless, all the same
tamquam	as if
tantus, tanta, tantum	so great
tempestās, tempestātis, *f.*	storm, season, violent disturbance

tempus, temporis, *n.*	time
teneō, tenēre, tenuī, tentum	hold
terreō (2)	I terrify
tertius, tertia, tertium	third
timeō, timēre, timuī	I fear, I am afraid (of)
tot	so many
tōtus, tōta, tōtum	all, the whole of, entire
trādō, trādere, trādidī, trāditum	I hand over, surrender
trahō, trahere, trāxī, tractum	I draw, drag
trānseō, trānsīre, trānsiī or **trānsīuī, trānsitum**	I cross, go through
tredecim	thirteen
trēs, trēs, tria	three
trīstis, trīstis, trīste	sad
trucīdō (1)	I slaughter
tū	you (singular)
tum	then
tumultus, tumultūs, *m.*	uproar, disturbance, riot
tūtus, tūta, tūtum	safe
tuus, tua, tuum	your (singular)
ualdē	to a high degree, very much, very
uastō (1)	I plunder, ravage, lay waste
ubi	when, where
uehemēns, uehemēns, uehemēns (*gen.* **uehementis**) (*adverb* **uehementer**)	vigorous, passionate
uelut sī	as if
uendō, uendere, uendidī, uenditum	I sell
ueniō, uenīre, uēnī, uentum	I come
uēr, uēris, *n.*	spring
uerbum, uerbī, *n.*	word
uereor, uererī, ueritus sum	I am afraid (of)
uertō, uertere, uertī, uersum	I turn
uester, uestra, uestrum	your (plural)
uetō, uetāre, uetuī, uetitum	I order ... not, I forbid
uiātor, uiātōris, *m.*	traveller
uideō, uidēre, uīdī, uīsum	I see
uidētur	it seems a good idea
uīgintī	twenty
uīlla, uīllae, *f.*	villa, country estate
uincō, uincere, uīcī, uictum	I conquer

uīnum, uīnī, *n.*	wine
uir, uirī, *m.*	man, husband
uirtūs, uirtūtis, *f.*	virtue, courage
uīs, *f.*	power, efficacy
uīsō, uīsere, uīsī, uīsum	I go to see, visit
uītō (1)	I avoid
uituperō (1)	I criticize, find fault with
uīuō, uīuere, uīxī, uīctum	I live
uix	scarcely
ūllus, ūlla, ūllum	any
undique	from every direction
ūnus, ūna, ūnum	one
uolō, uelle, uoluī	I wish, want, am willing
urbānus, urbāna, urbānum	belonging to the city, polished
urbs, urbis, *f.*	city
uterque, utraque, utrumque	each of the two
utī = ut (*but see* ūtor)	
ūtor, ūtī, ūsus sum + abl.	use
utrum ... an	(whether) ... or
utrum ... annōn/necne	(whether) ... or not
uulnus, uulneris, *n.*	wound
uxor, uxōris, *f.*	wife
Zēnō, Zēnōnis, *m.*	Zeno

Vocabulary: English–Latin

For use in the practice sentences

Macra (long markings) have not been given in this vocabulary. They are a guide to pronunciation, not part of the Latin words, and they should not be written.

a	*there is no indefinite article in Latin* (see p. 133)
about (= concerning)	de + abl.
admire	admiror (1)
afraid, I am	timeo, timere, timui
again	iterum; rursus
all	omnis, omnis, omne
allowed, I am	mihi licet, licere, licuit, licitum
always	semper
am	sum, esse, fui
an	*there is no indefinite article in Latin* (see p. 133)
and	et, -que
and ... not	neque *or* nec; neu *or* neue
angry	iratus, irata, iratum
any	ullus, ulla, ullum
anywhere	usquam
appear	uideor, uideri, uisus sum
approach	appropinquo (1) + dat.
arrive	aduenio, aduenire, adueni, aduentum
as if	quasi
ask	rogo (1)
at once	statim
avoid	uito (1)
battle	pugna, pugnae, *f.*; proelium, proelii, *n.*
beat	caedo, caedere, cecidi, caesum
because	quod; quia
become	fio, fieri, factus sum
bed, I go to	cubitum eo, ire, ii *or* iui, itum

before (conjunction)	antequam
beg	oro (1)
believe	credo, credere, credidi, creditum + dat.
best	optimus, optima, optimum
book	liber, libri, *m.*
both (= each of the two)	uterque, utraque, utrumque
boy	puer, pueri, *m.*
bring	fero, ferre, tuli, latum
brother	frater, fratris, *m.*
burn (set on fire)	incendo, incendere, incendi, incensum
but	sed, at
buy	emo, emere, emi, emptum
call together	conuoco (1)
camp	castra, castrorum, *n.pl.*
can	possum, posse, potui
capture	capio, capere, cepi, captum
catch	capio, capere, cepi, captum
chase	persequor, persequi, persecutus sum
cheap	uilis, uilis, uile
children	liberi, liberorum, *m.pl.*
city	urbs, urbis, *f.*
clever	ingeniosus, ingeniosa, ingeniosum
collapse	concido, concidere, concidi
Colossus	Colossus, Colossi, *m.*
come	uenio, uenire, ueni, uentum
command, I am in … of	praesum, praeesse, praefui + dat.
complain	queror, queri, questus sum
consul	consul, consulis, *m.*
country (= fatherland)	patria, patriae, *f.*
cross	transeo, transire, transii *or* transiui, transitum
dawn, at	prima luce
day	dies, diei, *m.*
decide	constituo, constituere, constitui, constitutum; mihi placet, placere, placuit
deed	actum, acti, *n.*; factum, facti, *n.*
depart	egredior, egredi, egressus sum
deserve, I … to	dignus (digna, dignum) sum qui + subjunctive
die	morior, mori, mortuus sum
do	facio, facere, feci, factum
don't	noli, nolite + infinitive

eager	cupidus + gen.
early	mane
embrace	amplector, amplecti, amplexus sum
emperor	princeps, principis, *m.*
encourage	hortor (1)
enemy	hostes, hostium, *m.pl.*; (*personal enemy*) inimicus, inimici, *m.*
even	etiam
evening	uesper, abl. uespere, *m.*
ever	umquam
every day	cotidie
every (with superlatives)	quisque, quaeque, quidque
everyone	omnes (= all people)
extremely	ualde
face	os, oris, *n.*
fall down	concido, concidere, concidi
fast	celer, celeris, celere
fatherland	patria, patriae, *f.*
fear	metuo, metuere, metui, metutum; timeo, timere, timui; uereor, uereri, ueritus sum
field	ager, agri, *m.*
fierce	acer, acris, acre
find	inuenio, inuenire, inueni, inuentum
fitting, it is … for me	me decet, decere, decuit
flee	effugio, effugere, effugi
foolish	stultus, stulta, stultum
for (= on behalf of)	pro + abl.
for some time	aliquamdiu
forget	obliuiscor, obliuisci, oblitus sum + gen.
forgive	ignosco, ignoscere, ignoui, ignotum + dat.
found	condo, condere, condidi, conditum
friend	amicus, amici, *m.*
friendly	amicus, amica, amicum
from	e *or ex* + abl.
general	imperator, imperatoris, *m.*
girl	puella, puellae, *f.*
give	do, dare, dedi, datum
give back	reddo, reddere, reddidi, redditum
go	eo, ire, ii *or* iui, itum
good	bonus, bona, bonum

greatest	maximus, maxima, maximum
Greek	Graecus, Graeci, *m.*
greet	saluto (1)
hang (transitive)	suspendo, suspendere, suspendi, suspensum
happy	laetus, laeta, laetum
harbour	portus, portus, *m.*
hard (= industrious)	diligens, diligens, diligens (gen. diligentis)
hate	odi, odisse
have in mind	in animo habeo (2)
he	is
help	iuuo, iuuare, iuui, iutum
her own	suus, sua, suum
here	hic
home	domus, domi *or* domus, *f.*
Homer	Homerus, Homeri, *m.*
hope	spero (1)
horse	equus, equi, *m.*
house	domus, domi *or* domus, *f.*
how long	quamdiu
husband	maritus, mariti, *m.*; uir, uiri, *m.*
I	ego
important, it is ... to	mea interest
in	in + abl.; (= into) in + acc.
in case	ne
in fact	re uera
inform	te certiorem facio (= I inform you)
into	in + acc.
it	id
Italy	Italia, Italiae, *f.*
kill	occido, occidere, occidi, occisum
king	rex, regis, *m.*
know	scio (4)
laugh	rideo, ridere, risi, risum
lead	duco, ducere, duxi, ductum
learn	disco, discere, didici
leave	relinquo, relinquere, reliqui, relictum
legate	legatus, legati, *m.*
lend	trado, tradere, tradidi, traditum
like	amo (1)

long (= for a long time)	diu
lot, a ... of	multus, multa, multum
love	amo (1)
lovingly	amanter
man	uir, uiri, *m.*; homo, hominis, *m.*
matter	res, rei, *f.*
midday, at	meridie
midnight, at	media nocte
money	pecunia, pecuniae, *f.*
more (= to a greater degree)	magis
much	multo
my	meus, mea, meum
never	numquam
no longer	non iam
no-one	nemo, neminis, *m.* or *f.*
now	nunc; iam
obey	pareo (2) + dat.
offend	offendo, offendere, offendi, offensum
one	unus, una, unum
orator	orator, oratoris, *m.*
order	impero (1) + dat.; iubeo, iubere, iussi, iussum
people	homines, hominum, *m.pl.*; populus, populi, *m.* (= population)
persuade	persuadeo, persuadere, persuasi, persuasum + dat.
picket	obsideo, obsidere, obsedi, obsessum
poem	carmen, carminis, *n.*
poet	poeta, poetae, *m.*
poetry	carmina, carminum, *n.pl.*
praise	laudo (1)
present	donum, doni, *n.*
prevent	impedio (4); prohibeo (2)
promise	promitto, promittere, promisi, promissum
quick	celer, celeris, celere
reach, I	peruenio, peruenire, perueni, peruentum ad + acc.
read	lego, legere, legi, lectum

realize	comprehendo, comprehendere, comprehendi, comprehensum
recital	recitatio, recitationis, *f.*
recite	recito (1)
remember	memini, meminisse
rest	quiesco, quiescere, quieui, quietum
return	redeo, redire, redii *or* rediui, reditum
Rhodes	Rhodus, Rhodi, *f.*
rich	diues, diues, diues (gen. diuitis)
Roman	Romanus, Romani, *m.*
Rome	Roma, Romae, *f.*; (in *or* at Rome) Romae
run away	effugio, effugere, effugi
sail	nauigo (1)
same	idem, eadem, idem
save	conseruo (1)
say	dico, dicere, dixi, dictum
scout	explorator, exploratoris, *m.*
sea	mare, maris, *n.*
see	uideo, uidere, uidi, uisum
self	ipse, ipsa, ipsum
senate house	curia, curiae, *f.*
senator	senator, senatoris, *m.*
send out	emitto, emittere, emisi, emissum
serious	grauis, grauis, graue
set out	proficiscor, proficisci, profectus sum
shame	dedecus, dedecoris, *n.*
she	ea
show	monstro (1)
sick	aeger, aegra, aegrum
since	cum
sister	soror, sororis, *f.*
so	tam (with adjectives and adverbs)
some(one) or other	nescioquis, nescioquis
sometimes	aliquando
soon	mox
spare	parco, parcere, peperci + dat.
speak	loquor, loqui, locutus sum
state	res publica, rei publicae, *f.*
stay	maneo, manere, mansi, mansum
still (= nevertheless)	nihilominus; tamen (2nd word)

street	uia, uiae, *f.*
stupid	stultus, stulta, stultum
talk	loquor, loqui, locutus sum
teacher	magister, magistri, *m.*
tell (= narrate)	narro (1) see also 'order', 'inform'
tenth	decimus, decima, decimum
than	quam
thank	gratias ago, agere, egi, actum + dat.
that	ille, illa, illud
the	*there is no definite article in Latin*
think	puto (1)
this	hic, haec, hoc
through	per + acc.
throw away	abicio, abicere, abieci, abiectum
town	oppidum, oppidi, *n.*
trust	credo, credere, credidi, creditum + dat.
try	conor (1)
two	duo, duae, duo
type, I am the ... to	is sum qui + subjunctive
unhappy	miser, misera, miserum
until	dum; donec
unwilling, I am	nolo, nolle, nolui
visit	uiso, uisere, uisi, uisum
walk	ambulo (1)
weather	tempestas, tempestatis, *f.*
well	bene
what	quid
what?	quid?
whenever	quotiens
where to?	quo?
where ... from?	unde?
where ... from	unde
where to	quo
where?	ubi?
wherever ... to	quocumque
whether ... or not	utrum ... annon *or* necne (necne *in indirect questions*)
whether ... or (conditional)	seu ... seu ... , siue ... siue ...
while	dum

who	qui, quae, quod
who?	quis?
whole	totus, tota, totum
wise	sapiens, sapiens, sapiens
with	cum + abl.
without	sine + abl.
woman	femina, feminae, *f.* ; mulier, mulieris, *f.*
word	uerbum, uerbi, *n.*
work	laboro (1)
write	scribo, scribere, scripsi, scriptum
year	annus, anni, m.
you (singular)	tu
young man	iuuenis, iuuenis, m.
your (singular)	tuus, tua, tuum

Benjamin Hall Kennedy's Memory Rhymes

The Public School Latin Primer by Benjamin Hall Kennedy, the headmaster of Shrewsbury, first appeared in August 1866. The Chairman of the Clarendon Commission, the body which investigated the nine leading English private schools in 1862–3, requested that their headmasters should consider commissioning a standard Latin grammar. (At the time these schools were using four different ones.) His fellow headmasters asked Kennedy, who had already written an *Elementary Latin Grammar*, to produce the new book.

His primer came in for severe criticism, raising a storm of correspondence in *The Times*. Thirty-six letters on (and somewhat off) the subject appeared there between 29 August and 9 November. The main complaints were that the primer was too difficult for young children, that the terminology was perverse and off-putting (Kenndey's use of the words 'trajective', 'prolative' and 'factitive' came under particular fire, and none of them is to be found in this grammar), and that the authoritative imposition of a uniform standard would be a serious blow to individual freedom.

A further cause of distress was that he had imported a new order of cases (nominative, vocative, accusative, genitive, dative, ablative). In fact, he was following in the footsteps of other British grammarians, but it was his work that has made this order standard in the UK, and therefore it is he who must take responsibility for the difference in practice in this respect on the two sides of the Atlantic.

Kennedy tinkered with his grammar over the next quarter of a century, for most of which time he was Regius Professor of Greek at Cambridge, and in 1888 his *Revised Latin Primer* was published. (In point of fact, it was largely 'ghosted' by his daughters Marion and Julia.) Apart from minor revisions, it has remained the standard grammar in the UK until the present time.

One feature of the primer which has generally met with approval is the inclusion of the gender rhymes that conclude it.[1] They will not to be everybody's taste, but they have a certain antiquarian charm, and those who learn them will have few problems with the gender of Latin words! We print them in tribute to a grammarian whose influence on the study of Latin in the UK has been unparalleled.

·····➤ [1] One of Kennedy's most dangerous critics in *The Times* correspondence was H. J. Roby, a rival compiler of a Latin grammar. His had been published four years previously. In his first letter to *The Times*, even Roby, apparently hunting for features in Kennedy's Primer which he could praise, remarked that the 'metrical jingle for the genders is well done, and, as I think, useful'. However, provoked by Kennedy's dismissive riposte, he complained in a second letter of 'the rhyming of long with short syllables in the metrical jingles'.

·····➤ In writing this short note, I have been much indebted to two books by Christopher Stray (*Grinders and Grammars: A Victorian Controversy* (Reading, 1995) and *Classics Transformed: Schools, Universities, and Society in England, 1830–1960* (Oxford, 1998)).

| General Rules

The Gender of a Latin Noun
by meaning, form, or use is shown.

1. A Man, a name of People and a Wind,
   River and Mountain, Masculine we find:
   Rōmulus, Hispānī, Zephyrus, Cōcȳtus, Olympus.

2. A Woman, Island, Country, Tree,
   and City, Feminine we see:
   Pēnelopē, Cyprus, Germānia, laurus, Athēnae.

3. To Nouns that cannot be declined
   The Neuter Gender is assigned:
   Examples fās and nefās give
   And the Verb-Noun Infinitive:
   Est summum nefās fallere:
   Deceit is gross impiety.

Common are: sacerdōs, dux,	*priest (priestess), leader*
vātēs, parēns et coniūnx,	*seer, parent, wife (husband)*
cīvis, comes, custōs, vindex,	*citizen, companion, guard, avenger*

adulēscēns, īnfāns, index,   *youth (maid), infant, informer*
iūdex, testis, artifex   *judge, witness, artist*
praesul, exsul, opifex,   *director, exile, worker*
hērēs, mīles, incola,   *heir (heiress), soldier, inhabitant*
auctor, augur, advena,   *author, augur, new-comer*
hostis, obses, praeses, āles, *enemy, hostage, president, bird*
patruēlis et satelles,   *cousin, attendant*
mūniceps et interpres,   *burgess, interpreter*
iuvenis et antistes,   *young person, overseer*
aurīga, prīnceps: add to these *charioteer, chief*
bōs, damma, talpa, serpēns, sūs, *ox (cow), deer, mole, serpent, swine*
camēlus, canis, tigris, perdix, grūs. *camel, dog, tiger, partridge, crane.*

Special Rules for the Declensions

First Declension (-a stems)

Rule—Feminine in First *a, ē,*
      Masculine *ās, ēs* will be.

Exceptions:

Nouns denoting Males in *a*
are by meaning *Māscula*:
and Masculine is found to be
Hadria, *the Adriatic Sea.*

Second Declension (-o Stems)

Rule—O-nouns in us and er become
      Masculine, but Neuter um.

Exceptions:
Feminine are found in *us,*
alvus, Arctus, carbasus,   *paunch, Great Bear, linen*
colus, humus, pampinus,   *distaff, ground, vine-leaf*
vannus: also trees, as pirus; *winnowing-fan, pear-tree*
with some jewels, as sapphīrus; *sapphire*
Neuter pelagus and vīrus.   *sea, poison*
Vulgus Neuter commonly,   *common people*
rarely Masculine we see.

| Third Declension (consonant and i stems)

Rule 1—Third-Nouns Masculine prefer
endings ō, or, ŏs, and er;
add to which the ending ĕs,
if its Cases have increase.

Exceptions:

(a) Feminine exceptions show
Substantives in dō and gō.
But ligō, ōrdō, praedō, cardō,   *spade, order, pirate, hinge*
Masculine, and Common margō.   *margin*

(b) Abstract Nouns in iō call
Fēminīna, one and all:
Masculine will only be
things that you may touch or see,
(as curculiō, vespertīliō,   *weevil, bat*
pugiō, scīpiō, and pāpiliō)   *dagger, staff, butterfly*
with the Nouns that number show,
such as terniō, sēniō.   3, 6

(c) Ēchō Feminine we name: *echo*
carō (carnis) is the same.   *flesh*

(d) Aequor, marmor, cor decline   *sea, marble, heart*
Neuter; arbor Feminine.   *tree*

(e) Of the Substantives in ŏs,
Feminine are cōs and dōs;   *whetstone, dowry*
while, of Latin Nouns, alone
Neuter are os (ossis), *bone*
and ōs (ōris), *mouth*: a few
Greek in os are Neuter too.   e.g. melos (*melody*), epos
(*epic poem*)

(f) Many Neuters end in *er*,
siler, acer, verber, vēr,   *withy, maple, stripe, spring*
tūber, ūber, and cadāver,   *hump, udder, carcase*
piper, iter, and papāver.   *pepper, journey, poppy*

(g) Feminine are compēs, teges,   *fetter, mat*
mercēs, merges, quiēs seges,   *fee, sheaf, rest. corn*
though their Cases have increase:
with the Neuters reckon aes.   *copper*

Rule 2—Third-Nouns Feminine we class
  ending *is*, *x*, *aus*, and *ās*,
  s, to consonant appended,
  ēs in flexion unextended.

Exceptions:

(a) Many Nouns in *is* we find
  to the Masculine assigned:
  amnis, axis, caulis, collis,   *river, axle, stalk, hill*
  clūnis, crīnis, fascis, follis,   *hind-leg, hair, bundle, bellows*
  fūstis, ignis, orbis, ēnsis,   *bludgeon, fire, orb, sword*
  pānis, piscis, postis, mēnsis,   *bread, fish, post, month*
  torris, unguis, and canālis,   *stake, nail, canal*
  vectis, vermis, and nātālis,   *lever, worm, birthday*
  sanguis, pulvis, cucumis,   *blood, dust, cucumber*
  lapis, cassēs, Mānēs, glīs.   *stone, nets, ghosts, dormouse*

(b) Chiefly Masculine we find,
  sometimes Feminine declined,
  callis, sentis, fūnis, fīnis,   *path, thorn, rope, end*
  and in poets torquis, cinis.   *necklace, cinder*

(c) Masculine are most in *ex*:
  Feminine are forfex, lēx,   *shears, law*
  nex, supellex: Common, pūmex   *death, furniture, pumice*
  imbrex, ōbex, silex, rumex.   *tile, bolt, flint, sorrel*

(d) Add to Masculines in *ix*,
  fornix, phoenix, and calix.   *arch, phoenix, cup*

(e) Masculine are adamās,   *adamant*
  elephās, mās, gigās, ās: *elephant, male, giant, as*
  vas (vadis) Masculine is known, *surety*
  vās (vāsis) is a Neuter Noun.   *vessel*

(f) Masculine are fōns and mōns,   *fountain, mountain*
  chalybs, hydrōps, gryps, and pōns, *iron, dropsy, griffin, bridge*
  rudēns, torrēns, dēns, and cliēns, *cable, torrent, tooth, client*
  fractions of the ās, as triēns.   *four ounces*
  Add to Masculines tridēns,   *trident*
  oriēns, and occidēns,   *east, west*
  bidēns (*fork*): but bidēns (*sheep*),
  with the Feminines we keep.

(g) Masculine are found in *ēs*
   verrēs and acīnacēs.   *boar, scimitar*

Rule 3—Third-Nouns Neuter end *a, e,*
   ar, ur, us, c, l, n, and *t.*

Exceptions:

(a) Masculine are found in *ur*
   furfur, turtur, vultur, fūr.   *bran, turtle-dove, vulture, thief*

(b) Feminine in *ūs* a few
   keep, as virtūs, the long ū: *virtue*
   servitūs, iuventūs, salūs,   *slavery, youth, safety*
   senectūs, tellūs, incūs, palūs. *old-age, earth, anvil, marsh*

(c) Also pecus (pecudis)   *beast*
   Feminine in Gender is.

(d) Masculine appear in *us*
   lepus (leporis) and mūs.   *hare, mouse*

(e) Masculines in *l* are mūgil,   *mullet*
   cōnsul, sāl, and sōl, with pugil. *consul, salt, sun, boxer*

(f) Masculine are rēn and splēn,   *kidney, spleen*
   pecten, delphīn, attagēn.   *comb, dolphin, grouse*

(g) Feminine are found in *ōn*
   Gorgōn, sindōn, halcyōn.   *Gorgon, muslin, king-fisher*

| Fourth Declension (-u stems)

Rule.—Masculines end in *us*: a few
      are Neuter nouns, that end in *ū.*

Exceptions:
   Women and trees are Feminine,
   with acus, domus, and manus,   *needle, house, hand,*
   tribus, Īdūs, porticus.   *tribe, the Ides, porch*

| Fifth Declension (-e stems)

Rule—Feminine are Fifth in *ēs,*
      Except merīdiēs and diēs   *noon, day*

Exceptions:
> Diēs in the Singular
>> Common we define:
> But its Plural cases are
>> always Masculine.

| List of Prepositions

| With Accusative

Ante, apud, ad, adversus,
Circum, circā, citrā, cis,
Contrā inter, ergā, extrā,
Īnfrā, intrā, iuxtā, ob,
Penes, pōne, post, and praeter.

Prope, propter, per, secundum,
Suprā, versus, ultrā, trāns;
Add super, subter, sub and in,
> When '*motion*,' 'tis, not '*state*,'
they mean.

| With Ablative

Ā, ab, absque, cōram, dē,
Palam, cum, and ex, and ē,
Sine, tenus, prō, and prae.

Add super, subter, sub and in,
When '*state*,' not '*motion*,' 'tis
> they mean.

Index

Words given in the **Glossary**, the **Some Tips** section, and the **Appendices** are only included here if they are likely to be consulted by those investigating the main body of the Grammar.